In the Middle of Nowhere
The History of RAF Metheringham

Text © Richard Bailey
Cover Illustration © Barrie Dunwell and **TUCANN***design&print*
All rights reserved. No part of this publication may be reproduced or transmitted in any form or by any means, electronic or mechanical, including any information storage and retrieval system without prior permission from the publisher

Produced by **TUCANN***design&print*
19 High Street, Heighington, Lincoln LN4 1RG • Tel & Fax: 01522 790009

CONTENTS

	Page
Introduction	3
Acknowledgements	4
1: A Satisfactory Satellite	5
2: Pro Libertate	13
3: Battle of Berlin	17
4: Prelude to Invasion	37
5: Support for Ground Forces	48
6: Return to Germany	60
7: The Second Winter	71
8: Anticipation	85
9: Victory in Europe	92
10: Preparations for Tiger Force	100
11: The Final Months	105
12: Epilogue	114
Appendix A: Station and Squadron Commanders	123
Appendix B: Operations flown from Metheringham	125
Appendix C: Aircraft and Personnel losses	131

INTRODUCTION

In writing this history of RAF Metheringham I have drawn heavily on the memories and experiences of the people who were there and lived through those wartime years, using official records to provide the bones on which to build their stories of life at one of the many bomber stations which sprang up in this part of England. This airfield rose from farmland and woodland and saw less than three years of intense operational activity before being quietly abandoned and reclaimed once more by nature and local farmers.

Many people have, no doubt, passed through the site of this once busy airfield unaware that RAF Metheringham ever existed. Those with an eye and a feeling for old airfields may have stopped to wonder what this place was. I was one of those who stopped, drove around the old perimeter tracks, stood on the decaying runway and wondered what life was like for those men and women who were stationed there.

I hope for those who were there that my small contribution allows others to understand something of what they did and what they achieved and to remember the sacrifices that so many of them made.

Richard Bailey
Walcott
February 1999

ACKNOWLEDGEMENTS

I wish to thank all of those who have helped and guided me during the past six years in gathering material for this book. I have received unreserved support from a great number of people, many of whom I have not been able to meet in person, but have corresponded with at length. I have been overwhelmed by their kindness and their willingness to share their memories with me. I apologise to those who do not see their story within these pages, it has been extremely difficult deciding where to 'draw the line' and to submit the manuscript for publication.

I particularly wish to thank Carolynn, my wife, for her patience and understanding; Jean for her constant encouragement and Andrew Clark for providing the initial motivation.

My thanks to:

George Aley, Dugald Armour, Alan Blue, Tom Bond, Stan Brickles, Ted Bullen, Harvey Clarke, Victor Cole, John Creasey, Rosie Creasey, Victor Cuttle, Robert Dack, Jack Dark, Bob Dawson, John Dawson, Fred Girkin, Gilbert Gray, John and Betty Greensmith, A D Groombridge, A V Hallett, John Harrison, Don Hodge, Harry Hudson, Harold 'Johnnie' Johnson, Betty Jones, Bill Kemp, John Lancaster, Jean Le Page, Ivor Llewellyn, Dave Merrett, Dick and Beryl Miller, George and Eileen Moulds, Ron Needle, Bill and Marion Oldham, Ron Patterson, WRP Perry, D Richards, Frank Richards, John Rogers, Peter Scoley, Bill Seymour, Eric South, Peter South, Harry Stunnel, Harry Turner, Bill Williams, A D 'Sandy' Wilson, Bill Winter, John and Mary Woodrow and Peggy Wright.

Chapter 1
A SATISFACTORY SATELLITE

In the summer of 1941 Britain had been at war for almost two years and, following the evacuation of the British Expeditionary Force from Dunkirk the previous summer, had seen 'The Few' hold out against the Luftwaffe to gain a hard fought victory in the Battle of Britain. America had yet to enter the War and Britain stood alone in the west against Nazi Germany. The only force capable of striking back at the heart of the enemy at this time was Bomber Command which, at last, was starting to receive deliveries of its new heavy bombers, the Stirling, Halifax, Manchester and ultimately the Lancaster.

There was now a desperate need for new airfields from which the heavies could operate, they were unable to use the existing grass airfields from which the variety of twin engined bombers operated and in any case there would be insufficient of these to meet the needs of the rapidly expanding bomber force. These new airfields were to be located in eastern England, principally in Lincolnshire, Yorkshire and East Anglia and potential sites were being evaluated.

One such site had been identified twelve miles to the south east of Lincoln, on the edge of the Fens, lying between the villages of Metheringham and Martin and alongside the B1189. In August 1941 the general site was surveyed and was found to consist of several agricultural holdings together with a mixture of woodland and scrubland with two lanes running almost east-west across the middle. The survey report concluded that *'with necessary tracking, grading and surface preparation and provision of an efficient drainage system, this site could be made into a satisfactory Operational Bomber Satellite.'*

Nevertheless an indication of the problems to come was given in a supplementary note *'the difficulty of draining the land must not be under-estimated'* although as the site was fairly level and about fifty feet above the

In the Middle of Nowhere - *The History of RAF Metheringham*

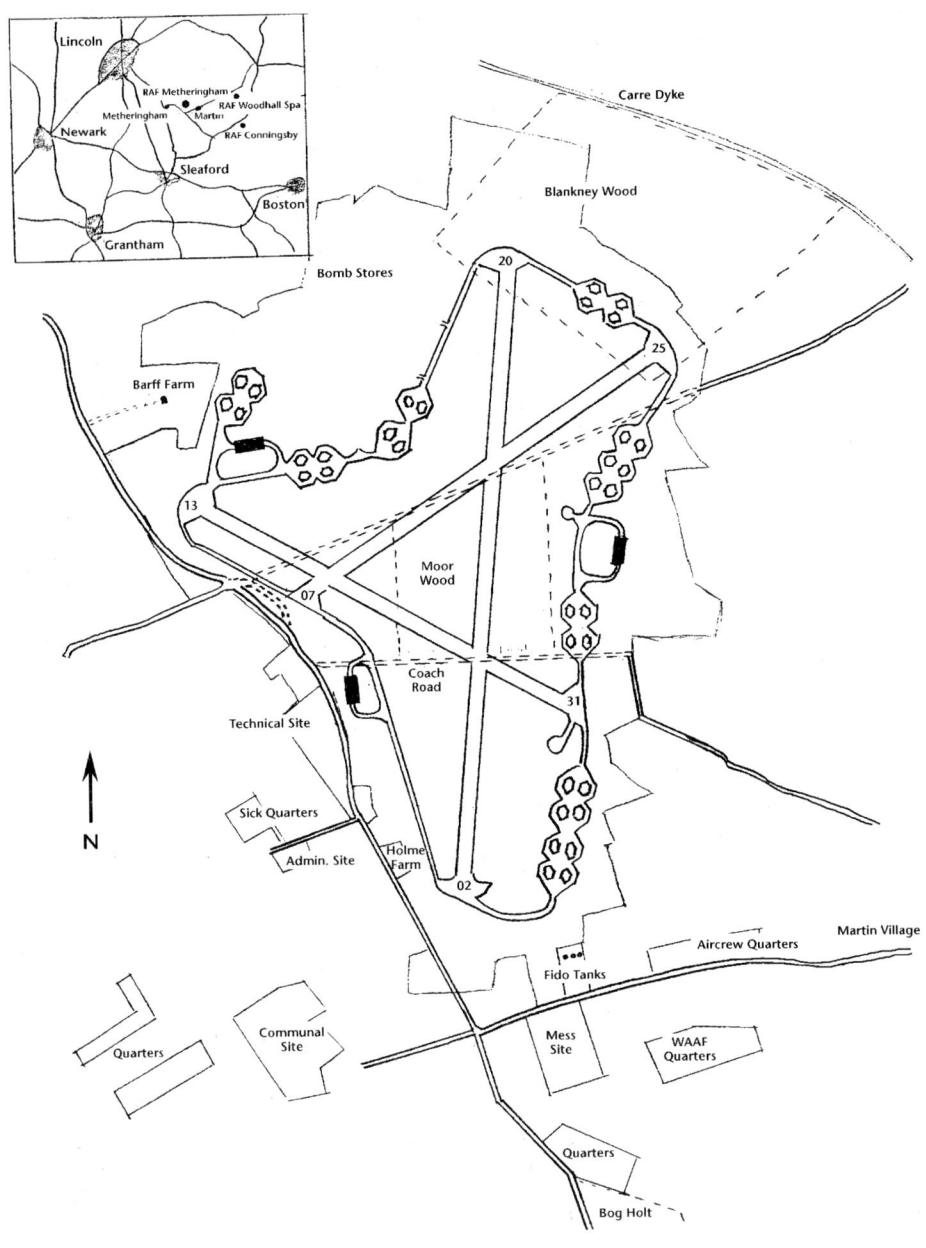

fens, only a few hundred yards to the south east, it was hoped that the only grading necessary would be *'cut and fill'*.

So it was then in September 1941 that local landowners were informed that the site was *'under review'* but that no decision had been made. There was some surprise amongst local people that the site should be considered at all, after all the 'powers that be' must be aware that the sub-soil in many places was running silt and would not support concrete runways and, with no further communication from the Director of Land & Requisition during 1941, it was assumed that the idea had been dropped. However in April 1942 the War Agricultural Executive Committee was informed of the intention to construct an aerodrome on the site and that *'requisitioning will proceed when final boundaries are determined but, in the meantime, owners and occupiers have been informed of the intention'*. Towards the end of June Notices of Requisition, under the Defence Regulations 1939, were formally issued. Responsibility for the construction works rested with the Air Ministry Works Directorate No. 17 Works Area at Belton near Grantham and in a letter to a local landowner an indication of the urgency for new airfields was given *'it is imperative that construction work should commence not later than the 27th July ..'*. Higgs & Hill were the main contractors with Carmichaels being sub-contracted to complete the runways, perimeter tracks and dispersed hardstandings.

So far the war had had little effect on this small community, in 1940 a searchlight detachment had been sited at the eastern end of the Coach Road whilst close to Barff Farm a decoy beacon, nick named locally 'flashing fanny', had sought to divert the attention of enemy aircraft from the fighter airfield at Digby four miles to the south west, proving successful on at least one occasion as bombs were dropped in the area causing minor damage but being quickly dealt with by the local ARP unit. The local Home Guard continued to patrol the area at night to guard against enemy infiltrators, returning to their labours within the predominantly agricultural community during the day.

The large areas of oak, ash and birch woods at Moor Wood and Blankney Wood provided an ideal setting for a Sunday afternoon walk, being a blaze of colour in the spring and summer with rhododendrons in profusion. Rabbits by the hundred were a traditional addition to the local diet and local poachers were tempted by the pheasants in Blankney Wood. One local man had a lucrative sideline trapping moles for their skins. This pleasant and picturesque part of Lincolnshire was about to change dramatically.

Peter Scoley, a schoolboy at the time, lived at Holme Farm with his parents who farmed much of the land which was to be taken. He recalls the arrival of the contractors with some dismay *'It was something of a shock to see the giant machines forcing their way through hedges and over dykes, wherever they felt like it, instead of using the gateways like our own tractors. The giant caterpillar tractors drove straight at the dykes, reared to an angle of nearly ninety degrees as tracks spun for grip then, as the grip came, down they would crash flattening hedge or fence in the process.'*

Moor Wood which stood almost in the centre of the new airfield site was quickly cleared and although a large area had previously been felled there was, according to the Air Ministry, three acres of good oak and ten to fifteen acres of mainly ash and fir this, together with timber from Blankney Wood and other areas on the site, was taken by the Ministry of Supply. One local farmhouse, earmarked for demolition, was approached by an avenue of chestnuts trees which were all felled, together with a single specimen of red elm which alone, without the benefit of chainsaws, took three men a day to fell yielding five hundred cubic feet of timber. Tom Bond, who lived nearby, recalls that the trees were cut down using cross cut saws, axes and wedges and that the 'chips' and smaller branches were made available to local people who eagerly collected them to supplement their coal ration. Many of the trees were of considerable age and the services of a shotblaster, Walt Sewell, from a local quarry were required to blast their roots from the ground. He lived in one half of a pair of cottages, which stood less than a hundred yards from the site for a bulk petrol store and which had initially been earmarked for demolition but were allowed to remain. Peter Scoley remembers that a great many of these roots were so large that the contractor's lorries could only carry one at a time as they were dumped either in the ' Bog Holt', to the south of the site, or adjacent to the Carre Dyke, to the north.

In place of Moor Wood there grew a giant concrete mixing plant fed by aggregate, from the local quarries to the west and north of Metheringham, and water pumped from Metheringham Beck and Carre Dyke and carried in tanks mounted on lorries to the plant. Bill Kemp, who worked for a wheelwright and undertaker in Martin village, remembered that workers came *'in their hundreds by 'bus and by train every day from as far away as Mansfield and Sheffield'*. The road to Metheringham was avoided by all local people first thing in the morning and last thing in the afternoon as the mass of workers made it's way to and from the railway station. Before long though hutted accommodation was available on the airfield and the dispersed living quarters were built which enabled the construction workers to live on site. From then on the two pubs in Martin, the Royal Oak and the Red Lion, were packed every night and Bill recalled the sight of *'two hun-*

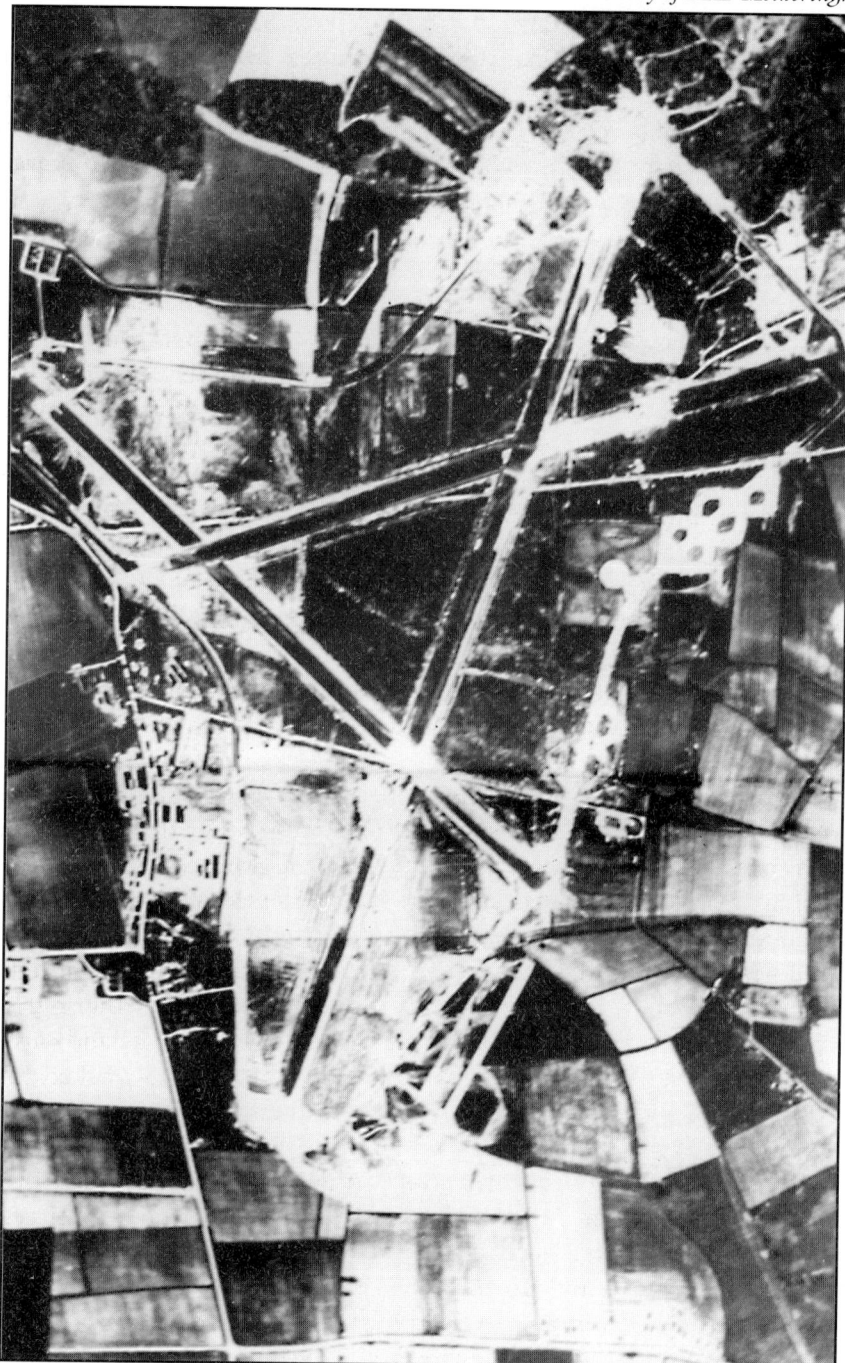

The airfield under construction - May 1943

dred drunken Irishmen weaving down Martin High Street singing 'Danny Boy' after closing time'. The contractors employed a welfare officer to look after them, he was billeted with Peter Scoley's parents, 'His job was not an enviable one, fights amongst his charges were common, broken heads the norm, the result of employing shovels and pick handles in many arguments. He bore it with equanimity and good humour and became a familiar figure roaring round the district on a powerful, noisy motorcycle, a thick cloud of oily smoke lingering in the air to mark his passing.'

As local people moved out of their requisitioned homes those not demolished immediately were put to use as temporary offices by the contractors until their site offices were completed, in a paddock to the north of Holme Farm. The Air Ministry queried whether Holme Farm would have to be requisitioned to make way for the perimeter track, in the event it was considered that the farm buildings would have to be demolished and the house vacated but on the 29 August 1942 it was recorded that possession would not be required immediately. Fortunately Peter's parents had been successful in finding an alternative farm but it would not be vacant until the spring of 1944, however they were told not worry as that timescale would be acceptable.

The problems which the locals had foreseen with the subsoil were now being discovered by the contractors. At the southern end of the site vast amounts of additional stone were needed to provide a stable foundation for the main runway and problems were encountered laying the sewers. The trenches, dug with a 'dragline' had no sheet piling to the sides which were thus unsupported, collapses were frequent and local knowledge suggests that at least one labourer, working in a trench, lost his life when the sides fell in. Similarly two horses stumbled into an unprotected trench, near to Martin Manor, one night and, unable to extricate themselves and despite efforts by local people to extricate them, they too perished. One story which has passed into local folk lore concerns a steamroller and a Caterpillar tractor which both sank into the silt, one trying to extricate the other, by the next morning they had both disappeared and there they are said to remain to this day.

American Army engineers arrived in the autumn of 1943 to install telephone cabling, laid in ducts in the roadside verges, to the various sites around the airfield. They wore heavy gloves covered with thick grease to enable the cables to slide through their hands as they paid out the cable from large drums. Peter and his brother had a thriving, albeit short-lived, sideline throwing apples over the fence from the family orchard to the Americans who in return threw back threepenny and sixpenny pieces. Seeing her winter store of apples rapidly disappearing his mother quickly put a stop to the enterprise.

During October 1943 Peter's parents received a telephone call asking why they were still there! The call concluded with the news that they must vacate their home by the end of the week as the house was required, fortunately they were able to lodge with Peter's uncle at Bracebridge near Lincoln. The reason for the sudden urgency became apparent as on the 20th October 1943 the airfield was opened on a Care and Maintenance basis, under the command of S/L Gordon DFC, as a satellite to RAF Coningsby. With its three intersecting runways it was a typical Class A wartime bomber airfield, the main runway of two thousand yards, aligned almost due north-south, with subsidiary runways of one thousand four hundred yards each. Although normally built to accommodate two squadrons the decision was taken, although no specific reason has been discovered, to house only a single squadron on the new airfield. Indeed in June 1943 the contractors had received instructions to abandon two RAF and two WAAF quarters sites, to complete one RAF quarters site as WAAF quarters and to convert buildings intended as Airmens and Sergeants Messes on the Communal site as quarters for Airmen and NCOs. Much of the land requisitioned for dispersed sites was therefore surplus to requirements and was duly handed back to its owners.

It had been generally assumed that the new airfield would be named after the nearby village of Martin, in the event it took its name from the larger village to the north west and became Royal Air Force Station Metheringham.

Pre-war aviation at Metheringham, a Flying Flea belonging to Mr Les Thorpe stands almost on what would become the threshold to Runway 13

Chapter 2
PRO LIBERTATE

At RAF Syerston, near Newark in Nottinghamshire, 106 Squadron shared the relative luxury of an airfield built to prewar standards with another heavy bomber unit, 61 Squadron, both flying AVRO Lancasters. 106 Squadron's origins lay with the Royal Flying Corps being formed in September 1917, initially flying RE8s, before re-equipping with Bristol F2Bs. However with the end of the war in 1918 there was no further role for this new Squadron and it disbanded only two years after its formation.

As the situation in Europe deteriorated new squadrons were being readied and 106 Squadron reformed in June 1938 at Abingdon in Oxfordshire, its Hawker Hinds soon being replaced by the Fairey Battle light bomber. Shortly after the outbreak of war the Squadron moved to RAF Finningley in Yorkshire and, having exchanged its Battles for Handley Page Hampdens, it became an advanced training unit and crew pool for the operational squadrons of 5 Group Bomber Command. Almost a year later the Squadron became semi-operational when it participated in 'gardening' sorties (laying sea mines) following which the posting of experienced crews gradually ceased.

The Squadron badge a lion sejant, rampant holding a banner charged with an astral crown, based on the crest of the County Borough of Doncaster close to RAF Finningley, was authorised in February 1941 the motto being Pro Libertate - For Freedom.

Once again the Squadron moved this time to RAF Coningsby in Lincolnshire where it became fully operational attacking Cologne, on 1st March 1941, together with a mixed force of Blenheims, Wellingtons and Whitleys causing damage in the docks area of the city.

Although the AVRO Manchester, the latest of the RAF's heavy bombers, albeit twin engined, had started to enter service in November 1940 the numerous problems which dogged this aircraft meant that by February 1942, when 106 Squadron received the Manchester in place of it's Hampdens, it

106 Squadron pictured after the 1000 bomber raid on Cologne on 30/31 May 1942, Guy Gibson at front centre and the Squadron's Manchesters in the background

had only seen limited squadron service and in fact 106 was the fifth squadron to receive the type. Nevertheless, having developed into a highly efficient and cohesive unit under the command of W/Cdr Robert Swinton Allen, DSO, DFC and Bar, the Squadron ensured a quick conversion to the type and on 20th/21st March took off on its first Manchester operation, 'gardening' off the Frisian Islands. Coincidentally on this same date (acting) Wing Commander Guy Penrose Gibson DFC, to become one of Bomber Command's most famous pilots, assumed command of the Squadron. Under his guidance 106 continued in its achievements and established itself at the top of the Bomber Command ratings. At the end of March it achieved the highest monthly tonnage of bombs dropped since the start of the war, the lowest aircraft loss rate and the lowest number of aborted sorties. Another first was achieved on 2nd/3rd May when the greatest number of Manchesters sent on one operation, eight aircraft, undertook yet another 'gardening' sortie.

In March 1942 it had been decided that all the heavy bomber squadrons of 5 Group were to be re-equipped with the new four engined AVRO Lancaster, although 106 were to soldier on with the Manchester for a further three months, their final operation being to Bremen on 25th/26th June. The Squadron's Lancasters had in fact started to arrive in May in small numbers, and took part in their first operation when eleven aircraft (and five Manchesters) joined the 1,000 bomber raid on Cologne on 30th/31st May.

Once again 106 set a new record when, in July, twenty one aircraft delivered sixty two tons of bombs to Dusseldorf, the greatest weight of bombs dropped by one squadron at this point in the war. The 10th September saw the Squadron leaving Coningsby, which was to close for the construction of concrete runways, and transferring to RAF Syerston from where W/Cdr Gibson relinquished command, in March 1943. It is well known that he was requested to form a special force, 617, Squadron to attack the Moehner, Eder and Sorpe dams. In forming this elite Squadron he was able to choose his own crews and in so doing selected amongst others F/Lt. J V Hopgood DFC and Bar, F/Lt. D J Shannon DFC and P/O L J Burpee DFM from 106 Squadron. The former B Flight Commander, W/Cdr. J H Searby DFC, took over the command of the Squadron maintaining the standards set by Gibson before being posted, shortly afterwards, to command a Pathfinder unit, No.83 Squadron.

It was then Wing Commander R E Baxter who led the Squadron during the Battle of the Ruhr and the Battle of Hamburg. In June 1943 photo reconnaissance pictures revealed the presence of what were thought to be rockets at a German research establishment on the Baltic coast, Peenemunde. This was seen as confirmation of previous evidence suggesting that rocket weapons were being developed for use against Britain and on the night of 17th/18th August Bomber Command sent a force of almost 600 aircraft to destroy this target. F/O J R C Hoboken of 106 Squadron achieved a bombing photograph which clearly showed his bombs falling directly over the aiming point. Immediately upon the Squadron's return from this operation the photograph was sent to Air Chief Marshall Sir Arthur Harris and, although the force as a whole had not succeeded in destroying Penemunde, once again 106's high level of performance had been clearly demonstrated.

RAF Syerston was now to cease its role as an operational station and in November 1943 both operational units received instructions to move, 61 Squadron to RAF Skellingthorpe, an already established wartime airfield just south west of Lincoln, and 106 Squadron to a satellite of RAF Coningsby, a new airfield - RAF Metheringham.

SECRET   No.5 Group Movement Order No. 11
Map References: Nil   COPY NO. _____
List of Appendices: Nil
                                Date   7th November, 1943.

Move of No.106 Squadron.

　　In consequence of the decision to vacate R.A.F. Station, Syerston, by Operational Squadrons prior to its occupation by a Conversion Unit, No.106 Squadron is to move from Syerston to Metheringham (Satellite to R.A.F. Station, Coningsby) on 9th November, 1943.

2.　The move is to commence on 8th November, 1943, and the Main Party and aircraft are to move on 9th November, 1943. The move is to be completed in such a way as will not interfere with the operational effort of No.106 Squadron and, if necessary, the above dates are to be modified in order to conform to operational requirements.

3.　All items of Squadron equipment laid down in Col.5 of War Equipment Schedule are to be transferred with the Squadron. No item of Squadron Barrack Equipment is to be included in the move.

4.　The Squadron is to move to establishment.

5.　Inspections with regard to marching out and marching in at R.A.F. Station, Syerston and R.A.F. Satellite, Metheringham, respectively, are to be carried out in accordance with K.R.& A.C.I. Para.1849.

6.　Headquarters, No.5 Group is to be informed by signal when the move is completed.

7.　ACKNOWLEDGE.

                                        Group Captain,
                                        Staff Officer i/c Administration,
                                        Headquarters, No. 5 Group, R.A.F.
5G/424/39/Org.

                                                    Distribution ....

Chapter 3
BATTLE OF BERLIN

Bomber Command was about to mount a prolonged offensive, commencing on 18th November 1943 and lasting until the end of March 1944, against the capital city of the Third Reich with the intention of destroying both it and the will of the German people to carry on the war. 106 Squadron had been given the task of maintaining operational status, for the forthcoming Battle of Berlin, whilst at the same time resolving the problems of bringing a new station into service. This would be a further test of the Squadron's ability and resources.

During the first week of November an advance party of five officers and sixty one NCOs and men, under the command of F/Lt H E C Keast, arrived at RAF Metheringham. They found a Station which was far from complete, in a state of 'organised chaos' with the contractors still on site, no electricity in many buildings, no water supplies to some sites and everywhere a sea of mud. For the first few nights all of the NCOs and men slept in the airmen's dining hall spending their days trying to turn the various sections into a fit state to receive the main party. Several of the flight buildings were lit using power from aircraft starter batteries until the electricity supply was eventually connected.

Aircrew had enjoyed their free nights in the local hostelries in Newark or, more often than not, Nottingham and being aware that a move was imminent most took advantage of the last opportunities to visit their favourite haunts. Sgt. Harry Hudson, flight engineer, having some free time on 10th November decided to pay a last visit to Nottingham. During that evening he met a young lady, from Devon, who was spending some time with relations in the city and who within two years would become his wife.

Movement order No 11 from 5 Group HQ instructed W/Cdr Baxter that the Squadron was to move to Metheringham on 9th November, although there was to be no interference with its operational effort. The

Lancaster JB593 ZN-T. The aircrew, left to right, are: George Remigio mid upper gunner, Ivor Llewellyn wireless op, Tony Romano bomb aimer, Reg Hinkley Pilot, Bob Blythe flight engineer, Jack Cooper rear gunner. Ground crew members unknown. Photographed by Joe Glazebrook, Navigator.

Squadron's Operational Record Book records *'Operations were again called for today and it was decided that the aircraft and ground crews should proceed to Metheringham and that the operation should be carried out from there. Three aircraft duly arrived but it was not possible to handle all the aircraft at the new Station at such short notice and it was accordingly planned to operate the other ten aircraft from Syerston. In the event, however, operations were cancelled and the Squadron aircraft flew over to their new base.'* F/Sgt. A D Groombridge's logbook shows that the Lancaster, in which he flew as the rear gunner was airborne for thirty five minutes for the transfer from Syerston, all of the crew's personal kit being stowed in the aircraft. Ivor Llewellyn, wireless operator with P/O. R Hinkley's crew, in the first aircraft to land at the new airfield recalls *'The runaway was camouflaged with an overlaid system of a light cream/brown substance which had the effect of breaking up the regular lines, we had been briefed about this before leaving our former base. On landing and still at speed on the long runway the aircraft bounced and slewed slightly, the cause was a thick pile of wood shavings, which were used to create the camouflage effect, having been left across the width of the runway. The following aircraft were held in the circuit while this obstruction was cleared.'* P/O W R P Perry in ZN-Z together with two other aircraft performed a mild 'beat up' of their new base to a chorus of 'The Java Jive' a song popular with the Squadron since Guy Gibson's time. Sgt Frank Richards, wireless operator, remembers arriving over Metheringham '...*to take in the view. 'It was a typical November day, overcast and wet, viewed from the air it didn't look too inviting. It was in the middle of nowhere and was our first sight of what was called a satellite airfield. On landing we booked in at the various sections and were shown to our quarters which were Nissen huts. After leaving a peacetime airfield this was, to say the least, a shock!'*

Immediately prior to the main party's arrival the new Station Commander had relinquished command of RAF Bottesford and transferred to Metheringham. G/Cpt. W N McKechnie, GC, accompanied by his wife, took up residence at Holme Farm only recently vacated by Peter Scoley's family. G/Cpt McKechnie had been a student at RAF Cranwell only a few miles to the southwest of his new command. It was there that, as a Flight Cadet in 1929, he had rescued a fellow cadet from certain death. A DH9A crashed on landing and burst into flames. The pilot although stunned managed to release his safety harness but fell out of the aircraft into a pool of blazing petrol. McKechnie had landed two hundred yards away and immediately raced to the scene and without hesitation ran into the flames and pulled the semi-conscious pilot to safety before extinguishing the flames on his clothing. McKechnie himself received superficial burns. For his actions he was awarded the Empire Gallantry Medal which as a decoration was replaced by the George Cross some years later, McKechnie exchanging his award at Buckingham Palace in July 1942.

Responsibility for the supply of ammunition, bombs and oxygen to the bomber squadrons lay with the Maintenance Units. 93 MU, which was to supply RAF Metheringham, operated from a site close to Swinderby railway station, near Newark, its storage areas continually extending to include many miles of roadside verges as the number of squadrons within Lincolnshire, and the scale of operations, increased. Cpl. Harry Turner was serving as a driver with 93 MU when instructions were received to commence deliveries of bombs to a new airfield, the location of which the staff at the MU were unsure. Being a local lad and knowing the area well it was Harry who led the first convoy of lorries to the bomb dump in what was left of Blankney Wood.

New aircraft were being delivered to Metheringham in preparation for the forthcoming assault on Berlin, these were Lancaster BIIIs fresh off the production line at Newton Heath, Manchester replacing the Squadron's BIs. Crews were soon distracted from the discomfort of their new 'home', with fighter affiliation flights, night flying exercises and equipment tests as well as local area familiarisation flights and, within a matter of days, G/Cpt McKechnie was able to declare the Station fully operational. 106 had come through once again and was able to put up thirteen aircraft for the opening raid on Berlin on the night of 18th/19th November. At the briefing for this the first operation from Metheringham W/Cdr 'Ronnie' Baxter calmly announced to the gathered crews *'Gentlemen - the Berlin season is now open'*

F/O Hoboken and his crew taxied out from their dispersal in Lancaster JB592, a new aircraft, about to make its third trip to the Big City, joining sixteen other Lancasters slowly making their way round the perimeter track before awaiting their turn to line up on the runway for take off. At 1730 the Lancaster laden with a 4000 lb cookie 1050 x4lb and 56 x30lb incendiaries accelerated down the runway, rose into the air and set course out over the North Sea. This was the night of 26th/27th November and the Squadron's fourth visit to Berlin within a little over a week. Limited nightfighter activity was encountered on the run in to the target due largely to a diversionary raid on Stuttgart and the German controller's incorrect assessment of the main target being Frankfurt, so that the only opposition over Berlin was flak. However on the return flight the nightfighters located the bomber stream and took their toll. F/O Hoboken was not heard from again after taking off from Metheringham.

John Lancaster, flight engineer, took part in the Squadron's fifth consecutive attack on the city on 2nd/3rd December. Unlike on the 26th/27th November on this night the nightfighters were waiting for the bomber force as it flew the long straight route towards the target and forty bombers were lost including one from 106. For John though the trip was uneventful and his main thought was *' This is a bloody fine way to spend my birthday!'* - his twentieth. After a raid on Leipzig the following night bad weather conditions precluded 'ops' for another two weeks, however this didn't prevent flying training continuing and at every opportunity crews were despatched on practise bombing and cross country flights to maintain their edge.

Once their period of duty had finished one of the main priorities for air and ground crews alike during this time was to return to their quarters and light the 'pot bellied' stove and to thaw out - trying to keep warm was almost a full time occupation. Coke for these stoves was rationed and the ration invariably used well before the next issue, this meant a clandestine operation, under cover of darkness, bucket in hand to the nearest coke compound where a hole in the wire fence indicated others were doing the same thing. LAC Bob Dawson, who had been with 106 since the Coningsby days, was fortunate enough to have the stove for his quarters at the bottom of his bed, which consequently proved to be a popular spot since the heat

from these devices did not carry very far in a Nissen hut. Bob, a Fitter 2E, recalls that about this time that they were adopted by a black and tan terrier *'She used to spend the morning on the perimeter track chasing any transport that might come past. At the end of her chosen beat she would snap at the rear nearside wheel then settle down to await a vehicle travelling in the opposite direction. This would continue all through the morning and afternoon with breaks for meal times when she would turn up at the mess hall and wait for any scraps that might come her way. We never knew where she spent the night but she was always on parade in the mornings.'*

Although entertainment facilities on the Station were limited at this time the NAAFI had been open from the beginning quickly becoming a focal point for social activities during off duty hours and offering light refreshments and hot meals. Moves were now being made for films to be shown courtesy of the Canadian Salvation Army. The local pubs in Martin, The Royal Oak and The Red Lion, were still packed in the evenings with labourers from the airfield so villages further afield were explored as of course was Lincoln, many airmen frequenting the well known aircraft haunt The Saracen's Head. Sgt. John Harrison visited the latter but recalls that his 'crew pub' was The Crown in Lincoln but they also took in the delights of hot toast, served with jam, and tea at a cafe in, or near, Boots.

An improvement in the weather allowed operations to resume on the nights of 20th and 23rd December and although on stand-by for 'ops' on Christmas Eve this was eventually cancelled and the Station Commander arranged for the various mess bars to be opened and the Yuletide celebrations began. Church services on Christmas morning were followed by the Airmen's Christmas dinner, turkeys, geese and *'lots of good fayre'* being traditionally served by the Officers with help from the NCOs. The day provided a welcome respite from 'ops' and was rounded off with a fancy dress ball in the NAAFI with music from the Station's dance band.

RAF Metheringham now had the benefit of its own Post Office which

MOC/C.   TELEGRAM EN CLAIR.   19/30.

                IMMEDIATE-NOTWT.

TO:-   43 GROUP SALVAGE OXFORD; 54 M.U. CAMBRIDGE;
       AM KINGSWAY; HQBC; HQ NO 5 GROUP; NO 106
       SQN METHINGHAM; RECORDS GLOUCESTER.

FROM:- COLTISHALL.

    RECD. A.M.C.S. 0601 HOURS, 30TH DECEMBER, 1943.

A625 30/DEC/1943 REPORTING F.B.

(A) LANCASTER AIRCRAFT MARK III No JD593.

(B) 106 SQUADRON METHINGHAM.
(C) COLTISHALL AERODROME 00.18 HRS 30/DECEMBER/43.
    DARK.
(D) FLIGHT ENGINEER SGT BRAID 97003 KILLED.
    WIRELESS OPERATOR P/O WORTH 158481 SLIGHT
    INJURIES TO ARMS. PILOT F/O ADSETT UNINJURED.
    NAVIGATOR P/O BLOY UNINJURED. BOMBADIER F/O
    CHLOH UNINJURED. MIDUPPER GUNNER P/O PAYNE
    UNINJURED. REAR GUNNER SGT HARRISSON UNINJURED.
(E) P/O WORTHY NORFOLK AND NORWICH HOSPITAL
    REMAINDER COLTISHALL.
(F) NORMAL BOMBER EQUIPMENT.

(G) AIRCRAFT DAMAGED BY ENEMY ACTION A. I. B. NO.

(H) CAT 'E' PROVISIONAL FUSELAGE AND MAINPLANE
    DAMAGE   E A SALVAGE NO.
(K) KINNOT.
(L) NIL.
                TIME OF ORIGIN:- 30/0400A HOURS.
CRASH CIRCULATION.
P.4. CAS. (10 COPIES).

SECRET   RAF STATION, METHERINGHAM.   APPENDIX 'A'.

SUMMARY OF OPERATIONS - NIGHT 1/2 JANUARY, 1944.

106 SQUADRON.

        Detailed   15
        Took Off   15
        Primary   12
        Missing   2
       - Outstanding 1

PRIMARY.   BERLIN Town Centre.

T.O.T. ordered for 4 a/c 0300-0304 Actual T.O.T. 0308-0309
                      3 a/c 0304 -0308   0315-0317
                      5 a/c 0308-0312   0313-0319
        12 Lancasters dropped 2x4000 Minol, 10x4000HE, 400x30lb, 10,800x4lb.

All crews bombed Wanganui flares which were few and scattered, and disappeared quickly into cloud. No results observed. V/106 claims one JU 88 damaged.

Weather 10/10ths cloud, tops about 18,000 feet.

MISSING.   F/106   No message received, bomb load 1 x 4000HC, 32x30lb, 900x4lb.
            J/106   No message received, bomb load as above.

OUTSTANDING. G/106   Landed at Bardney. -

- NOTE.   G/106 which landed at Bardney also attacked the primary, with 1 x 4000HC, 900x4lb and 48x30lb.

             - - - - - - - - - - - - -

                  Senior Intelligence Officer.

drew much favourable comment even warranting an entry in the Station's Operational Record Book - *'The official Station Post Office was declared open this day* (23rd December). *The Resident Engineer, who has taken a very full interest in this building, is to be congratulated on what is, without question, a very suitable Post Office.'*

The reality of war soon returned, 'ops' resuming on the 29th with another attack on Berlin. F/O ERF Leggett's crew flying in ED593 - Admiral Prune the Second, on its seventy third trip, had reached the target area unmolested by the flak defences, whilst bad weather had made it difficult for the German nightfighters to locate the bomber force. John Harrison, the rear gunner, recalls *' On the return leg we were hit by flak* (over Bremen) *which shattered the cockpit canopy killing the Flight Engineer outright and badly injuring the wireless operator in the right shoulder. We went into a screaming dive and I was stuck solid in the rear turret unable to move. Dickie, with the help of the Bomb Aimer, Chubby, managed to pull it out of the dive at about ten thousand feet. Both inboard engines were u/s, we had no wireless and both turrets were u/s. We were losing fuel but by throwing everything that was loose out of the door and hatches we managed to make Coltishall by the skin of our teeth. The Wireless Operator was taken to Norwich hospital.'*

During 1943 Bomber Command had begun to implement the Base organisation which grouped one or two-sub stations under a parent or Base station. Under this new arrangement each station assumed administrative responsibility for its resident squadrons and provided central maintenance facilities, both previously undertaken by squadrons individually. This allowed a reduction in squadron establishments which now comprised aircraft and aircrew with a small number of ground crew to meet operational needs and daily servicing, the Base station now undertook major servicing of all aircraft within the Base. On 1st January 1944 RAF Metheringham became a sub-station of 54 Base (number 4 Base within 5 Group), the Base station being RAF Coningsby and RAF Woodhall Spa the second sub-station.

New Years Day dawned cloudy and hazy with visibility improving under a stiffening breeze as fifteen aircraft were prepared for that night to continue the against Berlin. Despite the fact that nightfighter and flak defences were largely ineffective over the target area and overall losses were relatively light the New Year started badly for 106 with two aircraft failing to return. 'Ops' continued against the city, with the occasional diversion, throughout the remainder of the month.

An influenza epidemic, which had affected the Station almost since the Squadron's arrival, and which the Station Medical Officer attributed to the inclement weather and relatively hard living conditions had, at last, started to decline. People were now becoming acclimatised to the conditions and learning to make the best of their 'lot'.

Entertainments gradually improved in quality and quantity, the long promised films were being shown in the NAAFI courtesy of the Canadian Salvation Army and ENSA. F/Lt. Levy started a weekly record club, held each Sunday evening in the NAAFI, quickly building up a regular audience of classical music lovers. Similarly another group established the 'Brains Trust' loosely based on the popular radio programme of the time in which a knowledgeable panel of 'experts' answered questions on various topics from the audience. Concert parties from neighbouring stations were frequent visitors as well as units from other services an example being the Pipe Band of The Kings Own Scottish Border Regiment which *'..gave a stirring exhibition of pipe playing, sword dancing and Scottish songs in the NAAFI to an audience of four hundred'*, while the band from HQ Bomber Command, in concert in the Airmen's Mess and in the NAAFI attracted equally large audiences. Representatives from the YMCA were also looking at the possibility of providing a similar facility to the NAAFI and were investigating various sites close to the Communal site. Sports also played an important part in off duty recreation and the Station, even at this early stage, was able to field hockey, soccer and rugby teams competing in inter-section competitions as well as taking on neighbouring village teams, and nearby stations

Members of the MT section in font of a Matador fuel bowser

Victor Cole's crew celebrate after returning from the last 'op' of their tour. Left to right: Jock Haig wireless operator, Victor Cole, E Woods flight engineer (a replacement for the crew's own FE who was in hospital), 'Johnnie' Johnson bomb aimer, Malcolm Parkinson rear gunner, T Ross mid-upper gunner (the regular MUG J Harding was now a POW) and at the front, Alfie Bristow navigator

and squadrons.

Conditions were still proving difficult particularly for aircraft moving around the airfield. Unlike at Syerston, a wheel off the concrete at Metheringham meant sinking up to the axle in mud. On the night of 21st January members of the press were present to record the take off and return of the Squadron's Lancasters. As the first of A Flight's aircraft taxied round the perimeter track to the southern end of the main runway the third aircraft, on leaving its dispersal, put a wheel off the concrete and became firmly stuck in the mud partially blocking the perimeter track. Sgt. Dugald Armour recalls ' *We tried to get the next Lanc past but it was very tight and it too got stuck. It took some time to get the petrol bowsers in front to try to pull them out but we failed. Meanwhile the rest of A Flight and most of B Flight were arriving behind. As there was radio silence the pilots did not know what was happening. We had to talk to the skippers via the rear gunners. Engines were shut down and we pulled them backwards onto the short runway. In time a B Flight tractor arrived to help and we had to take trolley 'accs' to restart the* engines. Using sleepers and jacks we lifted the two aircraft out of the mud built a sleeper runway and pulled them on to the perimeter track.'

Only nine aircraft, of the sixteen detailed, managed to get airborne, one of these, ND331 G - George, had a problem with discharged batteries but was authorised for take off after a check on run-up. As G- George climbed out from Metheringham 'Johnnie' Johnson, bomb aimer with F/O. V Cole's crew, no doubt reflected on the previous night's 'op' to Berlin when night fighters found the bomber stream early on the way to the target. Tonight's 'op' followed a similar route to Magdeburg sixty miles south west of Berlin. He probably found time to reflect also on some of their previous 'ops' like the time they had broken cloud cover with a JU88 on their tail *'It was so far beneath us that the rear gunner was unable to align his guns on it. He gave the order 'corkscrew starboard' which was obeyed immediately by the skipper but the JU88's cannon shells hit the tail, part of the fuselage and the number one tank on the port wing. The pilot could not bring the aircraft out of the dive it was in and ordered us to prepare to abandon the aircraft. I released the front hatch, the pilot's hatch was released, when the automatic pilot pulled us out of the dive. We started to climb back to reach a safety margin of ten thousand feet in order to release the 4000lb bomb and incendiaries, as the flight engineer had ascertained that we had insufficient petrol to get to Berlin and back. I had just released the bombs when the rear gunner called out that we were well on fire in the fuselage behind him. It was then discovered that the 'fire' was the interior light which was switched on, that the rear door was open and that the mid upper gunner was missing. He ended up as a prisoner of war.'* Perhaps too Victor Cole recalled the views of his Flight Commander who maintained that his principal concern was with crews who had plenty of operations left to do. Nightfighters had found the six hundred and forty eight strong bomber force before it crossed the German coast and stayed with it all the way to the target area accounting, together with the flak defences, for fifty seven aircraft shot down. G- George brought its crew back safely. 'Johnnie' remembers *' We were the first crew to complete a tour of operations at Metheringham, in fact the first to complete a tour for over six months. S/Ldr Dunn our Flight Commander met us at dispersal with a crate of beer and the press photographed us by the side of G-George'*

For the first two weeks of February the Squadron stood down due to the moon period and although this gave a brief respite from 'ops' there was no let up in flying training, by night and day, much of which gave crews valuable practise in fighter evasion techniques. 'Ops' resumed on 15th February the target, once again, Berlin. All aircraft returned safely but whilst in the circuit over Metheringham the bomb aimer of JB534 called out *'air-*

APPENDIX "M"

Appendix to Form 540 for month ending 31st January 1944

Report on Health and Welfare of Personnel by Station Medical Officer

A rather large incidence of sickness is somewhat to be expected on a newly opened Station. Various factors have contributed to the production of such a state of affairs at Metheringham.
    Foremost amongst these was the "Influenza" epidemic. Fortunately it is now on the decline and does not constitute the same problem as in the first month or so, when shortage of hospital beds and poorness of transport facilities were acute.
    Next in importance must be cited the relatively hard living conditions as a result of the unfinished state and dispersed nature of the Camp. This is aggravated by its exposed site and the inclemency of the weather during the season. When assessing this it is of paramount importance to take into account the previous environment of the personnel affected.
    These personnel moved, more or less, "en masse" from more luxurious stations where more opportunities for entertainment both on and off the camp readily presented themselves. This sudden lowering of the standard of living, more apparent than real, sowed the seeds of discontent which magnified their hardships. It is, however, gratifying to see them become acclimatised to their new surroundings and make some attempt to help themselves. Nevertheless, the airmen's billets are still abhorred by some, and dissatisfaction is caused amongst Officers and N.C.O. Aircrew by the absence of baths, while the distance of the showers from their living quarters seems pointless.
    Station Sick Quarters is improving daily, the number of patient which can be accomodated being limited by shortage of nursing staff. Difficulty is being experienced in keeping meals warm which have to be transported some distance from the messing site.
    Despite the relative hardships which had to be endured during the breaking in" of the Station, the Squadron's operational effort speaks for itself and reflects credit on all personnel.

                      W. Meharg
                      Flight Lieutenant
                      Officer in Medical Charge,
                      R.A.F. Station, Metheringham.

```
Telephone No.: GERRARD 9234
Trunk Calls and    } "AIR MINISTRY," LONDON
Telegraphic Address }
```

AIR MINISTRY,
(Casualty Branch),
73-77 OXFORD STREET,
LONDON, W.1.

P.413926/7/P.4.A.2.

26 February, 1944.

Sir,

I am commanded by the Air Council to express to you their great regret on learning that your son, Sergeant John Cyril Harrison, Royal Air Force, is missing as the result of air operations on the night of 19/20th February, 1944, when a Lancaster aircraft in which he was flying as rear gunner set out to bomb Leipzig and was not heard from again.

This does not necessarily mean that he is killed or wounded, and if he is a prisoner of war he should be able to communicate with you in due course. Meanwhile enquiries are being made through the International Red Cross Committee, and as soon as any definite news is received you will be at once informed.

/If any

A. Harrison, Esq.,
 27, Brookside,
  Collingham Bridge,
   Near Leeds.

craft just in front' at which his pilot pushed the aircraft into a dive to avoid it. JB534 hit the ground at Timberland Fen and broke in two, all except the mid upper and rear gunners were killed. It would be almost another six weeks before the Squadron attacked the German capital city again.

From mid February the weather started to deteriorate with low cloud bringing in sleet and snow showers, on several occasions targets were detailed but then cancelled due to the unfavourable conditions. In one of the few breaks in the weather John Harrison settled himself into his rear turret in ME630 preparing for his tenth 'op', he had been to Berlin eight times, Frankfurt once and on this night, 19th February, was about to pay a visit to Leipzig. Diversionary raids on Berlin and minelaying in the Kiel Bay failed to draw away the nightfighters and the bomber force was intercepted as it crossed the Dutch coast and remained under constant attack all the way to the target. Adding to the already hazardous situation many aircraft reached the target area early, because wind speeds were not as forecast, and had to orbit until the Pathfinders arrived to mark the target. John's was one of the seventy eight aircraft lost on this raid. *' We were shot down by a ME110 just as we were making our last turn near Brunswick to head for Leipzig. The fighter attacked from underneath and slightly to the rear and, although I saw it, gave evasive action and opened fire, he managed to get a burst into the petrol tanks and also hit the fuselage towards the rear. We were unable to put the fires out and Dickie gave the order to bail out. The mid upper and myself tried to bale out from the rear exit but the door was damaged and would not open, so we had to make our way up the fuselage and go out by the front exit. I was the last to go and I saw that Dickie was still at the controls, he gave me a thumbs up sign and I felt him release my left flying boot which had got caught on something. Dickie* (Flying Officer E R F Leggett) *did not get out. Why I do not know. He looked alright but he may have been injured during the attack by the fighter, or the aircraft may have blown up before he got out. Whatever happened there is no doubt that he saved our lives by staying at the controls.'* John and the other five crew members became prisoners of war but it was some time before his parents found out that he had survived *'It was about a month after I was shot down that a neighbour was listening to Lord Haw Haw when he gave out my name and number.'*

By late February F/Lt Ginder's crew had completed twenty 'ops' and were selected to become one of the wind finding crews *'the wind direction and strength, calculated by the navigator, would be radioed back to be used in calculating an average figure for transmitting to all crews. We also flew as Pathfinder supporter, arriving with the first crews over the target with an all high explosive bomb load to subdue the defences. One such trip, to Schweinfurt*

(24th/25th February), *caused our one and only crew argument during an 'op'. A clear night, one of the first aircraft to arrive, and a perfect bombing run with visual identification of the aiming point. Our previous trips had not produced one really good photograph as fires, smoke or incendiaries burning had always blotted out the detail. This time it would be different! Soon the bomb aimer was calling "bombs gone" and was counting off the seconds as the pilot flew straight and level to await the photo flash. Suddenly a blue master searchlight picked us up, then another and another, until we were well and truly coned. The bomb aimer continued to count off the time for the photo flash, louder each time, as the rest of the crew, quite naturally, grew restive. Finally, in spite of the bomb aimer's protests the pilot dived away and jinked clear of the searchlights'*

Within the next few days the snow showers turned into heavy falls and soon covered the entire airfield to a depth of six inches. All available personnel, including aircrew, were pressed into service on snow clearing duties and by a supreme effort, in between snowball fights, succeeded in keeping the runways open even though this meant working through the night on more than one occasion. The Leap Year Dance organised by the WAAFs provided a very welcome opportunity to enjoy a break after all their efforts.

Daily servicing of the Lancasters continued at the dispersal points irrespective of the conditions and it was often the case that the 'erks' would devise their own procedures for carrying out maintenance tasks which were less time consuming than the official procedure and which, it must be said, did not jeopardise the high standards to which they constantly worked. As an example, to change the recognition lamp on the wing tip of a Lancaster officially required a tall trestle to be manhandled to a position under the trailing edge before climbing up it to reach the lamp unit. The usual practise, however, was to climb out of the upper escape hatch, to the rear of the astrodome, walk along the wing to almost to the end, crawling the final couple of yards and with feet hooked over the leading edge, head over the trailing edge and hanging on with one hand the lamp could be changed with the free hand. An A Flight electrician carrying out this procedure one day late in February found himself sliding off the trailing edge and somersaulting through the air. He landed in a heap of snow and walked away without injury, grateful for the recent snowfalls.

Operations were still being restricted by the weather and it would be mid March before they would resume in earnest. Meanwhile the contractors were making slow progress towards completing the Station, large areas of ground on the Technical site and the airfield itself required grading and seeding, an impossible task given the current weather conditions, the Station HQ and Sick Quarters remained unfinished whilst the Technical, Admin. and Squadron sites were still without a water supply. G/Cpt McKechnie maintained continual discussions with both the Resident Engineer and the Contractor but recorded that there were two hundred jobs outstanding which the Contractor had been asked to complete. In view of this lack of progress he decided that a programme of *'self help afternoons'* and *'camp nights'* when all personnel were to participate in cleaning and tidying up *'..should make a considerable difference to the appearance of the Station'*.

Dances were proving so popular that the NAAFI had been under pressure for some time to install a proper wooden dance floor and, although it would cost £100, it was argued that it would be well worth the expense. Eventually funds were forthcoming and during the two weeks it took to lay the new floor volunteers busied themselves hanging new curtains and painting and decorating the Institute. Upon completion a dance, organised by the WAAFs, proved a huge success and the new dance floor voted a great improvement rivalling *'...any Palais de Danse'*. Volunteers were also busy constructing a combined cinema and concert hall which would have the benefit of a stage, changing rooms and toilets. This would then allow more frequent film shows, removing the reliance on mobile film units visiting the Station, as well as offering improved facilities for touring concert parties and at the same time releasing the NAAFI for other activities.

There was a great deal of surprise and speculation when twenty American officers arrived at Metheringham early in March and even more so when British Airborne troops appeared overhead in gliders and gave an impressive display in landing their Horsas on the airfield. Ivor Llewelyn witnessed their arrival and was *'.... amazed at their steep angle of approach on landing.'* This was a hint of things to come as the Airborne were demonstrating glider techniques to the 9th USAAF Troop Carrier Command which would play a vital role in the movement of airborne troops in the forthcoming invasion of Europe.

From the time of its opening the Station's defences had been manned by members of the ground staff until early in 1944 when a detachment from 2756 AA Squadron of the RAF Regiment assumed the responsibility and, whilst there had been no real opportunity for them to prove themselves in action, regular exercises had been mounted to test their efficiency although these had invariably been curtailed because of operations. In mid March No. 3 Flight, 2751 AA Squadron arrived from RAF Strubby to take over from their predecessors.

On a raid to Stuttgart on 1st/2nd March a force of nearly five hundred and sixty bombers flew across France almost to the Swiss frontier before turning north east to the target area. Thick cloud on the outward and return routes prevented nightfighters from getting into the bomber stream and consequently losses were very light, four aircraft in total. Sgt. Frank Richards recalls that his pilot called him over the R/T to find out why, after repeated requests to the navigator for a course to fly to the target he wasn't getting a reply which made any sense. *'We could see bombs exploding miles away so we were totally off course. By this time the navigator was on the floor and seeing what was wrong managed to re connect his oxygen supply. By the time we got to the target everybody had left for home. We speedily bombed and got out, although the ack-ack had a jolly good try to get us. It was very close.'*

Although, because of the moon period, bomber 'ops' were now restricted a forecast of protective cloud cover over the south of Germany led ACM Harris to consider possible targets in this area for the night of 30th/31st March. Rejecting those targets on the priority listing he turned to possible Area targets one of which stood out as having received little attention for around seven months and which was, as a result, largely intact. The decision was made the target would be Nuremburg. P/O. E R Penman's, F/Sgt. T W J Hall's and F/Lt. C Ginder's crews were amongst the seventeen which 106 would contribute to this raid. Since their arrival at Metheringham in the previous November F/Lt. Ginder's crew had flown their 'ops' in JB601 V-Victor, a Lancaster III delivered new to Metheringham on the 6th of that month. The previous night they had taken V-Victor to attack an aero-engine factory at Lyons, their 29th 'op', this night though V-Victor was grounded with engine problems and for what was to be the final 'op' of their tour they were assigned ND682. F/Sgt Hall and his crew had flown the first 'op' of their tour only six nights earlier when they had attacked Berlin where they had made two runs over the target area before releasing their bombs. Having sustained flak damage to the engines over the target F/Sgt Hall managed to bring his crew home safely although the Lancaster was written off. Earlier this day his wireless operator, Sgt. Robert Dack had taken his washing to a lady in Martin village, who provided a laundry service to many of the aircrew, telling her that he would pick it up the following week. This night he would fly in JB566. Once airborne the bombers circled to gain height before heading for the assembly point out over the North Sea, from there the force headed for the Belgian coast. Nightfighters made their presence known a little after midnight as the force crossed the frontier into Germany and the first of the bombers started to fall, the target was still an hours flying time away.

Because the forecasted cloud cover failed to materialise the bombers were exposed in the clear moonlight and condensation trails pointed out

In the Middle of Nowhere - *The History of RAF Metheringham*

Harry Hudson, flight engineer, in the cockpit of JB601 ZN-V on 31st March 1944, he and the rest of Cyril Ginder's crew having completed their tour the previous night, although not in V-Victor

Sgt R McIntosh, second from right, and his groundstaff were responsible for servicing V-Victor

their route. Harry Hudson, F/Lt Ginder's flight engineer, watched *'bomber after bomber going down'* as they flew on towards the turning point north of Schweinfurt *'I looked back out of the blister at the side of the cockpit towards England, towards Plymouth where my girlfriend, Elsie, lived. I said out loud, with the intercom off," Goodbye Elsie, Goodbye Elsie." I quite reconciled myself to getting killed and after that I felt a great calm.'* JB566 was probably one of the bombers Harry Hudson saw going down. It was hit in the bomb bay and petrol tanks by a nightfighter. F/Sgt Hall ordered *'Its time to get out. Get out everyone.'* Robert Dack put on his parachute, which he always kept underneath his seat, but the Lancaster went into a dive and he was thrown on top of the navigator. *'I remember my face being pressed against two dials which were in the roof so I knew we were upside down.'* He tried to move the navigator up towards the front escape hatch conscious of the fact that *'....we had a blockbuster on board which went off on impact. I forgot that we wouldn't survive the impact ourselves. Then there was an almighty explosion and I was sent spinning. I thought we had hit the ground but it eventually dawned on me that I was in the air. Then something whooshed past my face and I was sitting nice and peacefully up in the sky under my parachute. I remember shouting for my wife, I was apologising because I had promised to be home on Saturday.'* Upon landing he sat at the foot of a tree and felt for his pipe and tobacco *' My boots and socks were gone but my pipe and tobacco were there so I sat there and smoked at least two pipefuls trying to think what to do next.'* He and the only other survivor, Sgt. C M Beston, the flight engineer, became prisoners of war and he never did return to collect his washing. F/O Penman's crew survived repeated attacks by a pair of nightfighters. With both turrets out of action and an engine on fire they managed to shake off the fighters and make for home. With difficulty they reached the emergency airfield at Manston where the undercarriage collapsed on landing, but they were safe.

F/Lt Ginder's crew being aware *'..that it was our last trip was already adding considerably to the normal tension! On the long straight leg that we flew through France and southern Germany we could see a larger than normal number of aircraft being shot down. We turned about a mile to the south of course and flew parallel, the pilot keeping up a gentle 'corkscrew' the whole way. This got us safely through and we went on to bomb Nuremburg, after first investigating some bombing being carried out at Schweinfurt in error. Safely back at base, telephone calls to our families and then off on leave'* before being posted to various units as instructors.

The attack on Nuremburg had been a failure, far from destroying the city only minor damage had been caused. Schweinfurt, which had been attacked by some aircraft in error, likewise suffered only minor damage. It had cost Bomber Command ninety six aircraft (one hundred and eight including those crashing in England on their return). 106 Squadron had lost three aircraft plus one written off, seventeen men killed and four prisoners of war.

The war was now about to enter a new phase and Bomber Command would switch to attacking targets in support of the landings in France with German industrial centres becoming secondary objectives.

Chapter 4
PRELUDE TO INVASION

During March 617 Squadron, based at RAF Woodhall Spa, under the command of W/Cdr Leonard Cheshire had been perfecting a new target marking technique with the help of 106 Squadron. 106 provided six experienced crews whose task was to precede the 617 aircraft, locate the target area and illuminate it with flares. W/Cdr. Cheshire then flew in at low level dropping markers and identifying the target for the remaining aircraft and, remaining in the target area, correcting any inaccurate bombing. The effectiveness of this technique was proven on 5th/6th April when W/Cdr. Cheshire, flying a Mosquito, successfully marked at low level an aircraft factory at Toulouse for one hundred and forty four Lancasters of 5 Group. The resultant bombing, being of near perfect concentration, severely damaging the target. As a result of this raid ACM Harris allowed AVM The Honourable Ralph Cochrane's 5 Group to operate as an independent force using its own marking techniques to the annoyance of AVM Donald Bennett, 8 Group Pathfinders. Two Lancaster squadrons 83 and 97, seconded to 8 Group, were returned to 5 Group together with one of 8 Groups Mosquito units, 627 Squadron. 83 and 97 Squadrons transferred to RAF Coningsby and 627 Squadron joined 617 Squadron at Woodhall Spa.

Traditionally officers and other ranks were quartered on separate sites and although this was how the quarters sites had been provided at Metheringham, when an additional site was ready for occupation in April it was decided that the officers and men of the Servicing Echelon should share the same site. This would no doubt be of operational benefit as well as maintaining the team spirit which the Station Commander did his utmost to promote.

One of the features of a wartime dispersed station was the considerable distances between the various sites, the service issue bicycle being essential

A Flight mechanics, left to right: Bernard Miles, Howard Main (tanker driver), Hank Nicholson, Nicky Guy, Paddy Donnachie (Flight Office Staff), Stan Brickles, Geoff Burton and Vic Taylor

to get around. LAC Bob Dawson's quarters were some distance from the maintenance hangar where he worked. *'This meant that one got up at the usual ungodly hour and cycled to the mess hall. After breakfast it was back to the domestic site to leave your utensils and then back over half a mile to the hangar. It kept one fit if nothing else.'* The bicycles were also extremely useful, when off duty, for reaching 'watering holes' in villages further afield than the nearby Martin and Timberland. Despite the blackout cyclists were still required to show lights on their bicycles which led to some conflict with the local police. Sgt Frank Richards recalls *'There was a time when a friend from 83 Squadron came over from Coningsby and we cycled down to a pub in Metheringham. At the end of the evening we left the pub, picked up our bikes and set off back to the Station. Unfortunately we hadn't put our lights on. A large Wolseley car came alongside and we were stopped by the local police. He proceeded to tell us that of course we were at fault for not having our lights on. To our amusement he said " Do you realise you could be killed riding without lights". We were risking life and limb most nights of the week every time we were on a raid and not only that we didn't see many cars in the evening down the country roads. Well he took our particulars and some time later we were summoned to appear in Lincoln court on a charge of riding without lights. I couldn't appear on the date stated as I was briefed to go on a raid. I received a letter to say I had been fined for the offence. My friend didn't pay his fine as he failed to return from that raid.'*

Not all of the local police were quite so rigorous though and LAC Stan Brickles remembers that after visiting the Wilson Arms in Walcott he would often ride back to the Station without lights accompanied by the local 'bobby'. He also recalls a well used ruse to explain a late return from a night out. *'The service police were always on duty at the cross roads at the entrance to the Station and we had to be in by 2359. If I was late I would cycle to within about a quarter of a mile then let a tyre down and walk the rest of the way and claim I couldn't help being late because of a puncture'* LAC John Greensmith, an engine mechanic, had used the same ruse many times. He was courting a local girl and spent a lot of his off duty time at her parents house at Walcott Fen, the home cooking making an enjoyable change to the food served in the Airmen's Mess. After a night out her parents would often make him up a bed for the night and John would cycle back to the Station in the morning to arrive at breakfast time. He was then able to cut across a field to the Mess site and from there return to his billet from the 'right' direction. On one occasion he was cycling to duty in the maintenance hangar and enjoying a cigarette, unfortunately G/Cpt. McKechnie caught him and promptly gave him a spell on 'jankers'. John recalls Cpl Rigluth who *'..was in charge of a gang of four fitters, he wouldn't entertain painting bricks and so on around footpaths but if a Lancaster required an engine change his gang was invariably called upon to do it. When replacing an engine it was usual practice to align the mounting bolt holes using ones finger, that is until Cpl Clements lost the end off his finger, then shortly afterwards a special tool was produced'*

Thanksgiving Day, Sunday 23rd April, was marked by a Church parade and joint service conducted by the Reverends Hichens and Wilson, 54 Base padres. After the service the congregation witnessed *'a very pleasing and special ceremony namely the christening of David Angus Kincaid, the second child and heir of our Station Commander.'* The infant was carried to the altar by Section Officer I M Pemberton, WAAF Administration Officer, accompanied by Mrs McKechnie and the christening performed by the Rev Hichens. Following the ceremony guests gathered on the lawn of the Station Commander's residence to drink a toast to the child.

The gymnasium had finally been completed and proved a popular attraction for many, particularly for those keen on badminton. Part also served as a Roman Catholic church partitioned by screens at its northern end, but the whole of the gymnasium could be used for church services if required. A purpose built squash court was also well used and although only initially available to officers, steps were soon taken to allow its use by aircrew members of the Sergeants' Mess.

From the time that Air Chief Marshall Harris had become Bomber Command's Commander in Chief he had pursued a strategic offensive against German industry and cities, maintaining a firm belief that this was the best and most effective use of his force in bringing about the defeat of Germany. Although he had, at times, been required to target other objectives, for example submarine pens, he had always resisted any diversion from his principal objective. However, when Bomber Command was placed at the disposal of General Eisenhower, along with the US Strategic Air Forces, ACM Harris protested strongly at what he believed was an abandonment of the offensive against Germany. Nevertheless his objections were overruled and Bomber Command was allotted a major role in attacking railway and communications targets in France and Belgium as well as military camps, ammunition dumps and armaments factories. Although he was doubtful that the precision necessary to hit this type of small target could be achieved and also concerned about the potential heavy casualties amongst the civilian population he gave his full support to the directive he received and spared no effort in ensuring that his Command carried out its task effectively.

Aircrews were themselves very keen to help prepare the way for the invasion armies and to be attacking targets which were of a more obvious military nature. The unfortunate aspect of which they were also only too well aware was the unavoidable losses amongst civilians in the occupied countries. In the event the attacks on the designated small targets were more successful than anyone, including ACM Harris, had expected and casualties amongst civilians were fewer than had been anticipated, but were nonetheless regrettable.

When not required to attack targets in preparation for the invasion the Squadron's Lancasters continued, as part of 5 Group's force, to attack German cities. These attacks were, however, infrequent and only undertaken when conditions were favourable, and with far fewer aircraft than had taken part in the recent attack on Nuremburg. Schweinfurt was earmarked for such an attack on the night of 26th April using, for the first time, the Mosquitoes of 627 Squadron as low level target markers and with 106 Squadron contributing sixteen Lancasters. Prior to flying on 'ops' the pilot from a newly trained crew arriving at an operational squadron would fly as a second pilot with an experienced crew, before taking his own crew on 'ops'. Sgt. Roy Bradley and his crew had only recently joined the Squadron and this night he was to fly as 'second dickey' with S/Ldr. A O Murdoch in V-Victor, JB601. Sgt Norman Jackson, flight engineer, had joined 106 whilst still at Syerston and although he had completed his tour he had volunteered to accompany his crew who had yet to finish theirs. He had only just

APPENDIX 41 (Contd.)
TO OPERATIONS RECORD BOOK
APRIL, 1944.

1. CRICKET. In the first round of the Group Competition we opposed Spilsby at home, and the game has been arranged for Sunday, May, 14th.
As the 5 Group League, proposed in March, has not been found practicable, a programme of friendly games with neighbouring Stations is being prepared.
Our Home Games will be played on the Martin Village Field, and on the airfield. A practice wicket has been prepared on the airfield, and a number of enthusiasts have already been out with bat and ball.
In addition to Station games an Inter-section Cricket League has been organised.

2. SOFT BALL. To meet the demands of Canadian Personnel on the Station, it is intended to run a team to compete in a Soft Ball League being organised by the Canadian Salvation Army, Digby.

3. TENNIS AND BOWLING. Facilities exist in the nearby village of Metheringham for tennis and bowling, and arrangements are being made by the Station for those interested to play there during the season.

4. NETBALL. A Netball pitch has been prepared for the W.A.A.F. on the Messing Site and fixtures are being arranged for the summer months.

5. SWIMMING. An open-air Swimming Pool is available at Woodhall Spa and it is hoped to include periods for Metheringham in the time-table.
During April a weekly visit has been made to the South Park High School, Lincoln, where personnel have had the opportunity to swim and do dinghy training.

6. THE GYMNASIUM and SQUASH COURT.
The floor of the Gymnasium was sand-papered and stained during the last week of April, and had to be closed while the work was in progress. It will be reopened on May 3rd. Upto the time of closing, the Gymnasium was in popular demand nightly for badminton and recreative physical training.

learned that he had a new born son as he prepared for the night's 'op' to Schweinfurt with F/O. F Mifflin as his pilot. Strong head winds had delayed both the target markers and the main force on their way to the target and nightfighters had located the bombers and were inflicting severe casualties. The low level marking was inaccurate and most of the bombs dropped fell outside the town resulting in little damage.

F/O Mifflin's aircraft ME 669 was leaving the target area at a height of twenty thousand feet when cannon shells from a nightfighter started a fire in the starboard wing adjacent to a fuel tank. Sgt Jackson although wounded in the right leg and shoulder by shell splinters decided to try to extinguish the fire. Pushing a fire extinguisher inside his jacket and fastening on his parachute pack he climbed out of the cockpit escape hatch. Almost immediately his parachute opened spilling the canopy and rigging lines into the cockpit. Nevertheless he continued as the pilot, bomb aimer and navigator gathered up his parachute, paying out the rigging lines as he slowly inched himself along the fuselage. He slipped and fell onto the wing managing to hold onto an air intake on the leading edge but losing the extinguisher in the process. By now the fire had spread and his face, hands and clothing were severely burnt. He lost his grip and was swept through the flames and off the trailing edge dragging his parachute behind him. Seeing his predicament his crew could only let go of his parachute and, despite the fact it was burning and only partially deployed, it held together and he made a heavy landing sustaining a broken ankle. At daybreak, his right eye closed and his hands useless due to burns, he managed to crawl to a nearby village where he was taken prisoner. He was to spend ten months in hospital recovering from his injuries. Meanwhile the pilot ordered the rest of the crew to bale out, four of them landed safely, F/O Mifflin and his rear gunner died in the aircraft.

JB601 suffered a similar fate being shot down near Laneuville-a-Bayard in France, Sgt Bradley was the only survivor and, badly injured, was looked after by the Resistance before being captured. Five of 106's Lancasters failed to return from this attack on Schweinfurt

Two weeks later the Squadron contributed twelve aircraft, of a force of fifty nine, to attack an ammunition dump at Salbris. The target was easily located and bombs were seen dropping onto buildings causing a great deal of damage. Although the defences were described by returning crews as being *'limited to one heavy gun'* and only one enemy aircraft had been seen over the target area nevertheless this attack cost 106 Squadron four Lancasters, out of a total loss of seven from the attacking force, including F/O ER Penman and his crew, who had barely made it back from

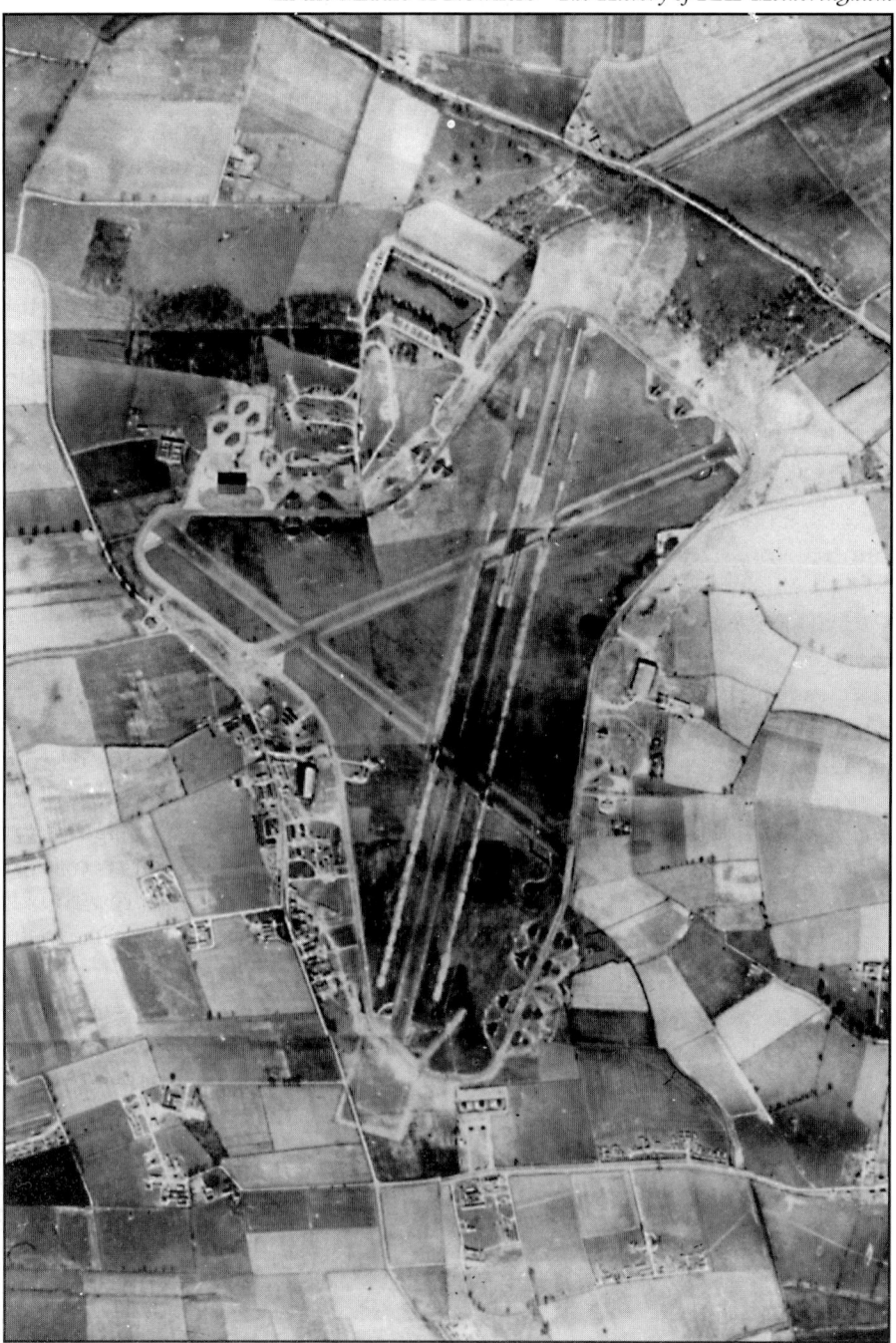

An aerial view taken in March 1945 showing FIDO in operation on the main runway (crossing the road for a short distance at the southern end)

Nuremburg six weeks earlier.

Although well placed for mounting attacks on occupied Europe the east coast airfields were susceptible to fog causing many casualties through flying accidents and a substantial loss in flying hours due to either its presence or the threat of it forming. Prime Minister Winston Churchill had become increasingly concerned at the danger presented by fog to aircrew and had instructed the Petroleum Warfare Department to find a method of dispersing fog at airfields, the name given to the project was Fog Investigation Dispersal Operation - FIDO. Tests showed that by installing petrol burners along both sides of a runway sufficient heat could be generated to 'burn off' fog and with careful design produced very little smoke. It was also confirmed that burners were required for the whole length of the runway and across the threshold for dispersal to be effective. Early in 1944 the decision had been taken to install FIDO at Metheringham, the second station in 5 Group to be so equipped, RAF Fiskerton's installation being operational in November 1943 (Fiskerton subsequently transferred to 1 Group in October 1944). By the middle of May the contractors, A Monk and Co., had completed the installation of all the pipe work and three large petrol storage tanks had been erected at the southern end of the airfield on the opposite side of the road to the Mess site. Petrol was pumped to these tanks via an under ground pipeline from a pumphouse at a siding, newly constructed to accommodate petrol tankers, at Metheringham railway station. To feed the generally low quality petrol to the burners pumps, powered by V8 engines, were housed close to the storage tanks. A full scale trial burning was carried out by the contractor between 1630 and 1700 on 18th May giving the opportunity for RAF personnel to man the installation under expert guidance. *'The story in Tee Emm Vol.4 No.2 re the pilot who, on returning from ops, thought he was over the target again was fully appreciated.'* is the description of the trial recorded in the Station ORB.

The following night the opportunity arose to try out the installation operationally when P/O CE Thompson returned early, from an attack on the locomotive workshops at Tours, due to R/T failure. Visibility had deteriorated to less than

Left to right: CE Thompson pilot, B Swinn wireless operator, J Harold mid-upper gunner, KD Goudman rear gunner, NS Forbes flight engineer, C White bomb aimer and D Elliot navigator

600 yards and, after he had made three attempts to land, FIDO was lit and, once the smoke had cleared, he was able to land without any further problems. The public road into Martin bisected the threshold to the southern end of the main runway and as a result when FIDO was in operation a wall of flame lined both sides of this road for a short distance. Peter Scoley, home on holiday from school, witnessed a test burning from close quarters on one occasion *'There was an armed sentry on guard that day. Seeing the road apparently blocked by two rows of monstrous fires my father stopped to ask the sentry whether it was safe, for he had not flagged us down. "I dunno" was the reply " But there's an officer just gone through in his car and he didn't catch fire, so I think its alright." We drove through without setting the car alight, but such was the noise and heat, that father thought it unwise to linger and drove quickly to emerge on the other side unscathed.'* F/O Victor Cuttle, wireless operator, even went through on his bicycle *' I just put my head down and pedalled like the clappers.'*

Soccer had been popular on the Station since it opened, there being plenty of space to set out a suitable pitch. Throughout the winter numerous teams had been competing in the Inter Section Soccer League and the Inter Section Soccer Knock Out, the final of which took place in mid May marking the end of the 'official' soccer season. A large crowd turned out to watch the Station Armoury beat the Electrical and Instrument Section by five goals to two. The Knock Out Trophy a *'handsome shield'* made in the Station workshop was presented to Aircraftsman Wale, the Armourer's captain, by Mrs. McKechnie. This represented a clean sweep for the Armourer's as they were also the League Champions. Attention now turned to cricket as the Inter Section League matches got underway, whilst the Station team appeared to be mopping up the opposition in the 5 Group Inter Station Knock Out. Competition in the Station's first athletic meeting on the first weekend in June was keen and well supported by an enthusiastic crowd. The Navigators' team narrowly beat the Pilots to take the trophy while individual winners were awarded prizes made up of War Savings Stamps and Certificates, again being presented by Mrs. McKechnie.

At last the 'Astra' cinema was ready for use, representing weeks of hard work by a substantial number of volunteers, although the tiered seating had not been installed, and it had to be admitted that the temporary chairs provided did prove rather hard after a time, its opening represented *'.... a highlight in the entertainment world of the Station.'* The grand opening film featured Roger Livesey in "The Life And Death of Colonel Blimp" *'...and although this was not exactly its premiere it was thoroughly enjoyed by all present.'* The sound and projection systems were *'excellent'* and really the only thing the cinema lacked were the peacetime neon lights. Such was its popularity that it was soon playing to full houses six nights a week. Sharing the same building the theatre was almost complete with only the stage lighting to be installed.

NO. 106 SQUADRON, R.A.F., METHERINGHAM.
ATHLETIC SPORTS MEETING.
AIRCREW INTER-SECTION

To be held on Tuesday 30th May 1944 or the first non-operational day after.

OFFICIALS

REFEREE: Flying Officer DUNNING.

JUDGES:
G/Capt. W.N. McKechnie CC
W/Cmdr. E.K. Piercy.
S/Ldr Taylor
S/Ldr Pearson
S/Ldr Leigh

F/Lt. S. Wilson,
F/Lt. Hardman.
S/Ldr G. Crowe DFC
Major A.S.C. Kennedy.

TIMEKEEPERS:
F/Lt Nash.
F/O Davies

F/O H.S. Nicholson DFC
F/O Goodman

STARTER: F/Lt. Lapham

MARKSMEN: F/O Newnes

F/O Carter.

ANNOUNCERS: F/Lt Keast

F/O Mack

RECORDERS: F/O Ibitt

Cpl. Higginson.

TELEGRAPH STEWARD: F/Lt Wray

LAP SCORER: P/O Whaley.

STEWARDS: F/Lt Sturdy

F/O Deans.

- 1 -

Chapter 5
SUPPORT FOR GROUND FORCES

The Allies had, for some time, been carefully putting into place plans which would lead the Germans to believe that any forthcoming invasion would take place in the Pas de Calais area, the shortest crossing point across the Channel. Although targets in Normandy had been attacked, the number and strength of attacks in the Pas de Calais area outweighed these by approximately two to one.

The Squadron's first 'op' in June had been against a railway battery at Marquise in the Pas de Calais area although only three aircraft had bombed, on the instructions of the master bomber, due to 10/10ths cloud covering the target area. Two nights later three Lancasters joined a small force to attack the Maisy battery situated between what would become the American landing beaches, Utah and Omaha. On the evening of 5th June sixteen crews were briefed for an attack on gun positions on the Normandy coast, at St. Pierre du Mont. Although they were not told of the significance of the operation they were to undertake their orders were unusual, no aircraft to fly below 6500 feet and no bombs to be dropped in the Channel. The reason soon became apparent as, when crossing the Channel en route to the target, a break in the cloud cover revealed a vast armada of ships of all kinds making steadily for the Normandy coast. Poor visibility hampered attacks all along the coast but, although the Germans were able to bring their guns into action, they had been so overwhelmed by the ferocity of the attack that the Allies were able to gain a foothold on the beaches. On this night Bomber Command dropped over five thousand tons of bombs and flew one thousand two hundred and eleven sorties, a record at this point in the war.

Caen which caused the Allies so many problems in the following weeks, was attacked on the following night to destroy two road bridges with 500 lb bombs. Smoke obscured the area and a delay in marking the target meant

Station Armourers...
...pose with a 'cookie'

that the bombers were waiting over a German strong point at a bombing height of three thousand feet, this together with considerable nightfighter activity resulted in the loss of two of the Squadron's Lancasters.

Throughout June 'ops' continued in support of the invasion forces breakout from the beachhead. The diversity of targets, which included ammunition dumps, oil storage depots and road and railway junctions, meant frequent last minute rearrangement or cancellation of 'ops' as circumstances affecting the ground forces constantly changed. Groundcrews, in particular, were hard pressed. Bomb loads were winched aboard then changed as the target changed and then they were changed again as the target reverted to the original. Cpl Harry Turner found himself delivering bombs direct to dispersal points and pushing 250 and 500 lb bombs off his lorry onto the grass alongside those which had already been loaded onto aircraft and taken off again. Time would be found later to return those which weren't needed to the bomb store. Cancelled 'ops' were also a source of frustration to aircrews. Sgt. Gilbert Gray, flight engineer, in a letter home wrote ' *What a mucking about we've had yesterday and today! Last evening, 'ops' were definitely off, then just as a load of fellows were preparing to go off the camp they were put on again and later they were finally scrubbed. Today has been the same. We were actually at the aircraft when they were cancelled. What a waste of time it is!*'

Out at the dispersals each Flight had its own office, a Nissen hut, divided into two, the smaller room with a desk, chairs and telephone was occupied by the Flight 'Chiefy' whilst the larger room housed six or so beds for the duty ground crew. Prior to 'ops' the Flight ground crew would be busy carrying out last minute repairs and systems checks and with a final check on oil and coolant levels before take off time. After take off the duty ground crew would retire to the Flight office, for a mug of tea or cocoa and stand by to receive the returning bombers in the early hours, after a night raid, or any aircraft which may have to make an early return, the duty senior NCO close by the telephone to receive reports from Flying Control, while the rest of the crew snatched some sleep. Part of their duty involved collecting lists of 'snags', from each aircraft's crew as they returned, for inclusion in the duty NCO's night log for rectification the following morning

George Moulds had recently moved, with his parents, to a house at the north eastern edge of the airfield adjacent to the B Flight dispersals and had become fascinated by the ceaseless activity of an operational airfield and by the Lancasters sat at their dispersals just a few yards through the trees from his parents house. At every opportunity he would sit and watch them being prepared for 'ops'. From his home he could hear the time for take off being given over the Station's tannoy system then, as the time approached, he would go and sit on a log to watch the engines being started, blue flames spitting from the exhausts in the gathering darkness. As the Lancasters taxied out to the perimeter track before wending their way to take their place in line ready for take off, the noise rose to an almost frightening level but soon all was quiet as the last aircraft rose into the air and disappeared into the night sky. Now he would go home to bed but early next morning would listen intently for their return and count them as one by one they touched down on the runway, how many had been lost tonight? When there was no one around George would venture onto the dispersals for a closer look at

Beatrice Harrad with her children. Rosie seated on the handlebars

the Lancasters, reaching up to touch the propellers, and gazing in awe at their size. Whilst rearming the turrets armourers would often throw part used belts of ammunition to the ground. George recalls that on many occasions he and his brother would hide one or two in a rabbit hole to be retrieved later for souvenirs, a practise which soon ceased after receiving the fright of their lives when they succeeded in setting off two or three rounds. Rosie Harrad lived in the semi-detached cottage next to Walt Sewell's close to the bulk petrol store and remembers her mother's concern for the aircrews *'She would be there to watch them take off and again when they returned, no matter what time of day it was.'* Both Mrs. Moulds and Mrs. Harrad kept chickens and found that, as eggs served in the messes were reserved for operational aircrews, the groundcrews were eager customers for their surplus supplies, Rosie recalls that they were fried on tin lids in the dispersal huts. In general the airmen were reasonably tolerant of the inquisitive children, Rosie managing rides on the bomb trolleys, but if they became too persistent steps were taken to discourage them. George whilst taking a short cut across the airfield on his way home from football was threatened with a spell in the guardroom and Rosie did see the inside of the guardroom, whilst waiting for her mother to collect her, having been caught playing on the airfield.

During off duty periods considerable effort went into raising funds for a multitude of different causes. Salute The Soldier week began in the second week in June with a target of £1500 to be raised on the Station, dances, raffles, auctions and other activities saw the amount raised exceed the target by a substantial amount. Where ever possible men and equipment were lent to neighbouring villages for exhibition at fetes and galas raising funds for such worthwhile causes as the Red Cross and the Air Crew Comfort Fund, amongst others. To raise funds for the 5 Group Prisoner of War Fund and to celebrate the fifth anniversary of the formation of the WAAF a party and dance, on 28th June, in the NAAFI seemed to be attended by almost everyone on the Station. A birthday cake specially made for the occasion by Corporal Robinson, chef to the Officer's mess, was almost too good to cut but S/O Pemberton finally performed the ceremony. All manner of schemes were devised to extract money from the party goers and by the end of the evening the princely sum of £34 7s 8d had been raised.

The final three night 'ops' of the month cost the Squadron five Lancasters, thirty three men killed. The two survivors were F/Sgt W R Knaggs, bomb aimer, and Sgt. W S McPhail, flight engineer, from F/O Wright's crew which attacked a flying bomb site on the night of 24th/25th June 1944. F/Sgt. Knaggs managed to evade capture for four months, eventually making contact with American troops of Lt.Gen. George Patton's Third Army, whilst Sgt. McPhail, having baled out, had the misfortune to land within the site being attacked. He was captured and taken to Gestapo headquarters for interrogation before being imprisoned at Abbeville eventually, after several moves, being interned at Salag Luft 7 at Kluczbork in Poland.

The 29th June saw the first daylight raid from Metheringham and 106's first since an attack on Milan on 24th October 1942. During the previous week crews had practised daylight formation flying and their aircraft had received distinctive tail fin markings, white with a green stripe, to aid in Squadron identification. At 12.20pm F/Sgt P Browne eased his Lancaster into the air, the last of fourteen to take off, making for the assembly point to rendezvous with the rest of the force before setting course for the target. After the anonymity and seeming security that darkness offered on night 'ops' it came as some surprise to be flying in the company of so many other aircraft and not a little disconcerting at how close they were. Sgt. Gilbert

LUCKY NUMBER..................

ROYAL AIR FORCE, METHERINGHAM.
28th JUNE 1944.

By kind permission of G/Capt. W.N.McKECHNIE G.C. ,

N O.   1 0 6   S Q U A D R O N

PRESENTS

W.A.A.F.   FIFTH   ANNIVERSARY   DANCE.

....
           At 20.10 hours the Squadron Commander,
Wing Commander E.K.Piercy, will pay atribute to the
           Womens Auxiliary Air Force.
....
Bar opens 19.30hrs.   Dancing from 2015 - 2359hrs.

ADMISSION : Silver collection will be taken at the
            entrance.
ALL PROCEEDS WILL GO TO THE PRISONER OF WAR FUND.

Programme....3d.

Master of Ceremonies - S/Ldr. G.Crowe DFC.

PROGRAMME

20.15hrs	Quickstep.		20.40hrs	Spot Waltz.
20.25	Paul Jones (Query - who is this guy?).		20.50	GRAND ELIMINATION DANCE - all instructions will be rigidly adhered to. The more the merrier - we'll soon clear you off the floor! Bags of fun guaranteed. PRIZES.
20.30	Envelope Waltz.			
20.40	Gents "Excuse Me" Medley.			
20.55	Foxtrot.		23.10	Slow Fox Trot.
21.05	Ladies "Excuse Me" Medley.		23.20	Conga. Palais Glide.
21.20	Quick Step - Toss the Coin.		23.40	Quickstep.
21.30	Tango.		23.50	the LAST WALTZ.
21.40	Old Fashioned Waltz.			- THE KING -

I N T E R V A L.
....
During the Interval, Section Officer Pemberton, with the ceremony befitting such an auspicious occasion, will cut and distribute the W.A.A.F.   BIRTHDAY   CAKE.

Light refreshments will be served during the interval and will be brought to you - so keep your seats and PLEASE do not waste any food.   Waste not, want not!

After you have been suitably refreshed, the Squadron will present a grand novelty feature - GUIDE THE BOMBER!!!   Definitely the first appearance in Metheringham!   Prizes for those who hit the target!

This will be followed by a topical "QUIZZ".   Teams selected from W.A.A.F. , Aircrew and Groundcrew will compete - more prizes.

........and now on with the Dance........

THE BAR will be open throughout the evening. One person will be served with not more than TWO glasses at any one time. We are not rationing you but experience shows that if you ask for four glasses you will drop at least one and upset another!
REFRESHMENTS - carefully concealed in a "wad" in a threepenny piece. Will you be the lucky one to discover it? - if you take it at once to the M.C.   You will get a surprise.
PROGRAMMES - a programme costs 3d. but you are not restricted to one. The more you buy, the greater will be your chance of winning a handsome prize. Remember, too, that your money will go to the Prisoners of War Fund.
PRIZES - will be presented as and when they are won.
A DARTS competition will be held in the Bar. Three darts for a 1d. Prizes for highest scores. No restriction on the number of throws.

WAAF's Fifth Anniversary Dance Programme

APPENDIX 80
TO OPERATIONS RECORD BOOK
JUNE, 1944.

REPORT ON STATION ENTERTAINMENT.
MONTH OF JUNE.

During the month of June there was a slight drop in the quantity and quality of live entertainment provided by way of stage shows, but to offset this, an increase in the number of dances.
 These play a valuable part in the social life of the Station and help to foster good relationships between all sections and ranks.
 The Station Cinema has been well supported, and has maintained a good standard of entertainment.

SUMMARY OF JUNE ENTERTAINMENT.
1. STAGE SHOWS.

(a). The Station Concert Party presented a revue "CHOCKS AWAY" on Friday, June 9th. This had the makings of a good show but lacked direction.
(b). On Friday, June, 16th. Tom Ratcliffe, the well known Community Singing Leader, paid a visit. With the rather small audience at his disposal, he achieved a fair measure of success but community singing has not a universal appeal.

(c). A lease-lend company organised by E.N.S.A presented variety on Friday night, June, 23rd, and staged a very attractive show, probably the best of its type which Metheringham has had up to the present.

2. MUSICAL CONCERTS.
(a) The Sunday Evening Gramophone recitals organised by F/Lt. Levy and F/O. Ibbit have continued. These concerts prove very popular to a small section of the Station personnel who attend faithfully every Sunday evening.

3. CINEMA SHOWS.

(a) The mobile units which served the Station well in the early days have discontinued their visits, as the Static Cinema operates six nights a week.
(b). The Static Cinema has maintained a good standard of films and generally speaking is very well attended.

4. OTHER FORMS OF ENTERTAINMENT.

One lecture was provided during the month, on Wednesday, June 7th. the speaker being Madame Biddulph.
 There was a poor attendance although the lecture had been widely advertised.

5. DANCES.

Dances have formed a considerable part of the month's entertainment and proved very popular.
(a) During "Salute the Soldier" week two dances were organised, one on June 8th. and the second on June 15th.
 They both provided the means of adding a substantial amount to the total of Savings.
(b) The Corporal's Club ran a Social and Dance on Thursday June, 22nd, and maintained the usual high standard.
(c) On June 28th. 106 Squadron organised a dance in aid of the Prisoners' of War Fund. S/Ldr. Crowe devised a very enjoyable programme of entertainment, part of which was devoted to a ceremony celebrating th 5th. Birthday of the W.A.A.F.

R.A.F. METHERINGHAM
By kind permission of G/Capt. W. N. McKECHNIE, G.C.

Presents

"CHOCKS AWAY"!

A Revue

PRODUCED BY

JOCK WILSON

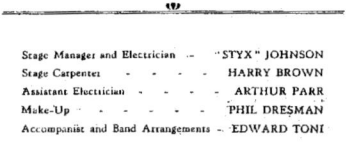

Stage Manager and Electrician - "STYX" JOHNSON
Stage Carpenter - - - HARRY BROWN
Assistant Electrician - - - ARTHUR PARR
Make-Up - - - - PHIL DRESMAN
Accompanist and Band Arrangements - EDWARD TONI

W. K. MORTON & SONS, PRINTERS, HORNCASTLE.

"CHOCKS AWAY"!

1. OVERTURE

2. ANYWHERE IN BOMBER COMMAND:
   Mary Angus, Winnie Collins, Joyce Grayson, Carol MacFarlane, Rita Sutherland, Jock Wilson, Bill McAlear.

3. CRAZY MOMENTS:
   Freddie Stewart, Vic Stewart, Ron Terry.

4. JOINING THE W.A.A.F   Bill Wray

5. MUSICAL MOMENTS,:   Freddie Palmer

6. MY SONG GOES ROUND THE WORLD:
   George Sandells, with Winnie Collins, Joyce Grayson, Carol MacFarlane, Mary Angus.

7. WONDERS AND BLUNDERS:
   Jock Wilson, Bill McAlear.

8. MELODY AND HUMOUR   Gwen Bouqet

9. THE SAUCY LAD   Phil Dresman

10. NOT ALL THERE   - -   Ted Redding

11. THE LANCASTRIANS:
    Leader, Stan Green; Clarinet, Stan Sharman; Violin, Jock Wilson; Piano, Edward Toni; Drums, Johnny Keatley.

12. L.D.A's. NIGHTMARE;
    Jock Wilson, Bill McAlear Alan Mack, Bill Wray.

13. SONGS AT THE PIANO: Tommy Pullen

14. SPECIALITY:
    Mary Angus, Winnie Collins, Carol MacFarlane, with Freddie Palmer, Rita Sutherland, Joyce Grayson.

15. SMILE AND A SONG   Pat Hobson

16. OPERA—TIONS
    Bill McAlear, Ted Redding, Phil Dresman George Sandells, Derek Freeman.

17. STILL CRAZY:
    Freddie Stewart, Vic Stewart, Ron Terry.

18. FINALE   The Company

Gray, F/Sgt Browne's flight engineer, recalls that '*On the way out it was reassuring to see the Spitfires wheeling above us. The sun glinted on their canopies.*' Although the fighter escort ensured freedom from enemy fighter interference flak was heavy and accurate. '*The flak was frightening. At night it was gone in a flash and the smoke which the explosion left was barely seen. It was very different in daylight when we had to fly through the smoke puffs waiting for the next one to come up! Very scary! Even more scary were the aircraft slightly above us. Near the target the bomb doors opened to reveal the load - 11 x1,000 pounders and 4 x500 pounders- and there they were just above us. I remember that just before the target we accelerated slightly to take us clear of the force so that we would not be bombed by our own aircraft.*' The day was clear but cloud at 15,000 ft obscured the markers. '*We had to bomb through the cloud on 'Gee'. We flew on the first wave and our bombs were dropped at 13.46 hours from 19,000ft.*' After an uneventful trip F/Sgt. Browne touched down two hours and fifty minutes after take off and the first aircraft back at Metheringham. Of his first daylight 'op' Gilbert Gray thought '*it was lovely up there and even at 19,000 feet I was sweating. Most of the time we were amongst towering cumulus clouds which looked quite attractive in the sunlight.*' Things hadn't been so uneventful for F/Sgt J Netherwood, over the target his Lancaster had been hit by flak damaging the hydraulics and both port engines, by skilled flying he nursed ND868 back safely to the emergency landing ground at Woodbridge.

F/O D Meredith and his crew had arrived at Metheringham earlier in June and for the remainder of the month undertook flying training, circuits and landings and cross country exercises, by day and night, and local area familiarisation flights. Some of these flights were in a strange looking Lancaster which had no bomb doors and a cutaway bomb bay, this was one of the Lancasters used by 617 Squadron on the Dams raid on 16th/17th May 1943, both AJ-J flown by F/Lt. D J H Maltby and AJ-G flown by W/Cdr Guy Gibson spent some time at Metheringham being used for training purposes.

The first two operations in July dealt a serious blow to 106 Squadron when seven aircraft failed to return, the target in both cases being a flying bomb storage site at St. Leu D'Esserent north of Paris. On the first of these F/O Meredith's crew were detailed to make their first operational sortie. He and fellow pilot F/O Mavaut were good friends and the two crews went to briefing and their pre 'op' meal together. The attack on this night, 4th/5th July met with fighter opposition over the target. F/O Mavaut's aircraft, ND682, was one of the victims '*..enemy aircraft was sighted starboard quarter up by rear gunner just before getting to target area. He warned* the pilot who started to corkscrew straight away. The enemy aircraft then turned in to attack from starboard quarter up with the moon behind it. The rear gunner opened fire at 800 yards just before the enemy aircraft fired, he saw tracer from the fighter pass just above his turret and then heard an explosion seemingly from inside the Lancaster, then a shower of perspex chips and a quantity of oil hit his turret. There was no reply from the mid-upper gunner when he was 'called up' and when one of the crew went to him he was unconscious having head injuries.' F/O Mavaut carried on and bombed the target, on return he landed at Woodbridge, Sgt. Ekins, the mid-upper gunner, being taken immediately to Sick Quarters where he died shortly after. It was found that a cannon shell had exploded in his turret.

The caves at St. Leu D'Esserent had been a source of building material for centuries, those to the north side of the mile wide Oise valley were still used for stone quarrying while those to the south had been used for growing mushrooms. However, over a period of two years the Germans had adapted the caves for storing flying bombs. Branch lines now linked the main railway to a network within the caves. Inside the floors were concreted and living quarters and canteens had been created, together with piped water and electricity supplies. This vast project required large numbers of French labour, providing an opportunity for members of the Resistance to infiltrate the work gangs, gain information and send detailed plans of the storage facility to London. It had been reported that the site had the potential to receive over seven thousand flying bombs a day. Three nights later, on 7th/8th July, the Squadron returned to seal the caves. Intense fighter opposition was encountered before reaching the target and continued until the force was on the return leg. P/O A Monaghan's Lancaster, ME831, was attacked and set on fire over Rouen, ten minutes from the target. The order to abandon the aircraft was given, the bomb aimer loosened the forward escape hatch but although it jammed he managed to get out. Sgt. Swinley, flight engineer, who followed was caught by the neck his body swinging in the slipstream and the fire drawing closer. He finally worked himself free and parachuted to earth, his neck bearing scars of the ordeal. All of the crew successfully escaped from the burning aircraft.

Not surprisingly many airmen found girlfriends from the surrounding villages, and from the Land Army hostel at Martin Manor in Martin village. For many the relationships lead to marriage and, as a result, a surprising number of airmen stayed, or returned after the war, to live in the area. Being in the countryside meant there were many quiet spots to be found for courting, one couple found a car, jacked up on blocks for the duration, in an old barn, whilst there were numerous convenient haystacks to be found! At this time there were around one hundred and fifty WAAFs on the Station and romances blossomed on the Station itself, indeed there were four marriages during July. In many cases, however these romances were short-lived where a boyfriend was aircrew and, at a time when few crews were surviving to complete a tour, it became almost inevitable that one or more young ladies would date a succession of aircrew boyfriends who would fail to return. Superstition would then point a finger at the unfortunate WAAF as a 'chop' girl. A newly arrived rear gunner on spending his first evening in the Sergeants Mess noticed a WAAF sitting by herself in the anteroom and looking quite lonely. On enquiring who she was he was advised to have nothing to do with her as everyone who had mixed with her in the mess, or had taken her out, had 'got the chop'. He didn't believe in the superstition and invited the young lady to join him and his crew for a drink. She eagerly accepted and they enjoyed a pleasant evening. The WAAF developed a close relationship with the crew's bomb aimer and they later married, he survived to complete his tour, albeit with another Squadron.

By now a new crew room was ready for use and volunteers from the Waafery helped to clean, polish the floors and put up curtains made in the Station's tailor's shop. To add a finishing touch cycling parties collected flowers from the surrounding countryside.

In a typical month, and despite the demands of operations, time was found for inspections of all the various functions of the Station. For example during July there were inspections by the Principal Medical Officer, Bomber Command; Flying Control, 5 Group; the Accounts Officer, 54 Base; the Catering Officer, Bomber Command; the Armaments Officer, Bomber Command and the Base Commander, Air Commodore Sharpe. The latter was particularly impressed ' *The general tidiness of the station its cleanliness, both inside and out, the various buildings, offices and sections have been brought to an exceptionally high standard. It is difficult to single out any particular section for special praise. The WAAF site, Sick Quarters, Gas Section and Servicing Wing must however receive a word of special commendation. I was much impressed by the enormous amount of work which has been done outside the buildings and sections in the way of gardens and general tidiness. It might appear at first sight that so much effort on exterior appearances must have been made at the expense of efficiency in operations and administration work but this was clearly not the case. It was quite obvious that all ranks take a great pride in the cleanliness and efficiency of their Station. A first class Station, I congratulate all concerned.*'

On the 30th July twenty one aircraft took part in an operation to bomb German positions opposing Americans in the Villers Bocage area at Cahagnes.

Because of cloud few aircraft were able to bomb and 106's aircraft were recalled. PB304, piloted by F/O P Lines, was seen to be in difficulties over Manchester and, in what was assumed to be an attempt to land his aircraft, which still had 18 x 500lb bombs on board, it crashed killing the crew.

The daylight raids in support of the ground forces continued into August. Flight engineer Gilbert Gray remembers *'On these summer days above the clouds it became very hot under the perspex in the greenhouse of the cabin and we were generally in shirtsleeves. My parachute was stowed so that, in hindsight, I was very vulnerable in the event of a sudden catastrophe! My engineer's tool kit served as a picnic hamper to accommodate the sandwiches and drinks (soft!) which were supplied while my escape kit, a small box containing rice-paper maps, chocolate, currency etc, was stowed there too. Escape photographs were under my Sergeants stripes. A threepenny piece was sewn under my brevet for luck!*

Attention turned, on 6th August, to the submarine pens on the Atlantic coast. Lorient was heavily defended and several aircraft received flak damage including F/Sgt Browne's which returned on three engines after losing the starboard inner. On landing coolant was discovered spouting from the port outer, which would not have continued running for much longer. Five days later his crew completed its tour, 34 'ops' with an attack on the pens at Bordeaux, Gilbert Gray recalls ' *We were one of six aircraft sent ten minutes ahead of the main force of thirty five Lancasters, which included 617 Squadron, to act as windfinders. We obtained a brilliant aiming point photograph of the U-boat pens.'* When these pens were captured a few weeks later the 2000lb armour piercing bombs had not penetrated the roof.

Chapter 6
RETURN TO GERMANY

A suitable site finally having been found and following several weeks of building works the long awaited YMCA opened to complement the facilities offered at the NAAFI and, although not as large, it provided a welcome additional source of hot meals and an alternative location for smaller scale social functions. Indeed F/O Ibbitt, the Station Gas/Fire Officer, transferred his Sunday night recorded music sessions, which he had taken over from F/Lt Levy in April, there from the NAAFI. G/Cpt. and Mrs. McKechnie attended the opening ceremony and within a few minutes the building was filled to capacity.

At Nocton Hall, only five miles from RAF Metheringham, the Americans had established the Seventh General Hospital. Originally acquired by the Air Ministry at the outbreak of the war, as an extension to the RAF Hospital Cranwell, Nocton Hall was found to be unsuitable, the facility consequently being transferred to the mental hospital at Rauceby, near Sleaford. Used by the Army as a casualty clearing station until 1943 the Americans then took over Nocton Hall in 1944 in the expectation of substantial numbers of casualties from the invasion forces in Normandy. C-47s had become familiar visitors to the Station, from June onwards, as they ferried in casualties from the continent for transfer by ambulance to Nocton Hall, where they received first line aid before being flown from Metheringham to Prestwick or Renfrew in preparation for the Atlantic crossing and home.

G/Cpt McKechnie had continued to fly operationally whenever the opportunity arose, usually with a new or inexperienced crew, although as the Station Commander he was not required to do so. He also made regular use of a Tiger Moth, acquired as personal transport, in which he would often perform early morning aerobatics over the airfield, a sight well remembered by those stationed at Metheringham at that time. Mrs.

McKechnie too had become a familiar figure around the Station regularly attending social and sporting events and presenting prizes for all manner of competitions. She was also frequently to be seen helping to dispense tea and biscuits amongst the aircrews on their return from 'ops'.

From the middle of August attention turned, once again, to targets in Germany, the first being to Stettin where considerable damage was caused to the port and industrial areas. On the night of 29th/30th August the Squadron was to make a second attack on Konigsberg, an important Baltic supply port for the Eastern Front, having already undertaken the round trip of almost two thousand miles three nights earlier. G/Cpt McKechnie had elected to fly with a relatively inexperienced crew his aircraft would be JB593. Over Konigsberg the bombers endured a twenty minute delay until the marker aircraft found a break in the low cloud obscuring the target. The attack was extremely successful, largely due to the very accurate marking, and the red and green target indicators were *'plastered'* destroying almost half the housing and a fifth of the industrial area, the resulting fires were visible for one hundred and fifty miles on the return leg. Considerable nightfighter opposition had been encountered over the target and over the Baltic and the Squadron lost two Lancasters, one was JB593 with the Station Commander and his crew. On return to Metheringham crews were stunned to learn of the loss and all hopes were that he had landed away. Sadly this was not to be. W/Cdr Piercy, 106's CO, temporarily took over command of the Station and recorded in the Station ORB ' *The Squadron has greatly benefited from G/Cpt McKechnie's long flying experience and his advice, always cheerily given, was much sought after. His huge enthusiasm for operations and his readiness to fly on every possible occasion was an inspiration to every member of the Squadron. He was particularly admired for the way in which he always insisted on operating with a new or inexperienced crew. His loss from a pilot's view alone will be a bitter blow and his spirit will long be remembered with the utmost respect.'* G/Cpt M L Heath assumed command of the Station on 5th September.

F/O Meredith's crew were carrying out pre-flight checks on their aircraft in preparation for an attack on the Luftwaffe's airfields in Holland. His two gunners Sgt. D Hodge, mid-upper, and F/Sgt M Bruce, rear, stood beneath the open bomb bay doors examining the load to be delivered. Suddenly a 1,000 pounder fell from its shackles, struck F/Sgt Bruce a glancing blow to the head and crashed to the ground. Startled but otherwise uninjured the two gunners immediately warned the rest of the crew before sprinting away from the dispersal, spreading the warning to other crews as they went. The Armaments Officer duly arrived, replaced the fuse and instructed the armourers to load the offending bomb back into the Lancaster with a parting shot to the crew not to bring it back. They duly obliged and dropped it on Deelen airfield.

In the early hours of 19th September the Station was shaken by a tremendous explosion. Immediate investigation ruled out any incident on the Station and no aircraft were in the vicinity, ruling out a crash. The cause was eventually found to be a flying bomb which had come down in a potato field at Tanvats, about one and a half miles away. The V1 had been observed crossing the coast, at Skegness, at 0413 hours falling to earth seven minutes later having covered twenty eight miles. Damage was slight, a few broken windows in nearby farmhouses and a crater, twenty five feet in diameter and six feet deep, in a field of potatoes.

Since relinquishing command in March 1943 W/Cdr Guy Gibson had maintained contact with his old Squadron, more especially since becoming Base Operations Officer for 54 Base and being stationed at Coningsby, as his duties often brought him to Metheringham. Now holding a non-flying post he had nevertheless managed to gain the necessary authority to fly as Master Bomber for a raid on Rheydt on the night of 19th September. He flew a Mosquito of 627 Squadron, orbiting the target, calmly giving bombing instructions to a mixed force of 1 and 5 Group Lancasters. Two of 106's aircraft did not return from this raid along with W/Cdr Gibson, and his navigator S/Ldr J B Warwick, who were both killed as their Mosquito crashed in flames near Steenbergen in Holland. One other 106 Lancaster encountered problems as it returned to base, its pilot unable to locate the airfield or make contact by radio. In avoiding another aircraft PB298 hit a tree, rapidly losing flying speed it crash landed in a field at Brandon near Fulbeck fifteen miles to the southwest of Metheringham. All of the crew were taken to Newark General Hospital before being transferred to the RAF Hospital at Rauceby. All had received cuts and abrasions and were suffering from shock but were otherwise all right except the mid-upper gunner who had suffered head and chest injuries.

Although there had not been a recurrence of the 'flu epidemic which struck the Station during the first few months, nevertheless the exposed nature of its location, with very little shelter from the winds and rain, meant coughs and colds were a routine feature which, by the majority of personnel, could be shrugged off and caused little interference with their normal duties. However where such an infection occurred among aircrew it normally meant a spell off 'ops' until it had passed since other complications could arise, with a resultant effect on operations. As an example one aircraft, of sixteen despatched in late September on a raid to the Dortmund-

Ems canal, had to abandon and return early when its mid-upper gunner lapsed into unconsciousness due to the effects of eustachian catarrh, his disability deprived the crew of a vital look out thereby rendering the aircraft vulnerable to attack from fighters. This same raid also marked the end of their tour for F/O Meredith's crew and, despite being attacked by a nightfighter, and their aircraft damaged, they returned safely after a round trip of four hours and fifty minutes.

Towards the end of the month a full Station parade saw the AOC 5 Group, The Honourable Ralph Cochrane, present a Silver Lancaster trophy to 106 Squadron. The trophy had been donated to 5 Group by A V Roe Ltd, to be presented to the squadron in the Group with the least number of avoidable aircraft accidents over a three month period. 106 were the first holders and held it for three consecutive periods. At the presentation the AOC accorded well deserved praise to the ground staff for their often overlooked part in keeping the Squadron flying.

Another facet of bomber operations unfolded at the end of September as the nineteen aircraft, Hurricanes, Spitfires and Martinets, of 1690 Bomber Defence Training Flight flew in from RAF Scampton to join the strength of RAF Metheringham. The Flight's role, under its CO S/Ldr J L Munro, being to provide training to 5 Group's bomber crews in fighter defence and evasion techniques. It had formed at 106's old base, Syerston, earlier in the year.

106 Squadron itself took on a new role, that of 'nursery' for future 5 Group Pathfinder crews. 5 Group ORB records, in September 1944 '*A new method was introduced for selection of crews for PFF Squadrons attached to the Group and No. 106 Squadron is, in future, to be the 'nursery' for these squadrons. Crews earmarked for PFF duties, while under training with the Group are to be posted to No. 106 Squadron to operate in the normal way until they are required in No. 83 or No. 97 PFF Squadrons. A carefully selected team of specialists and experienced Flight Commanders has been set up in No. 106 Squadron to ensure a sound background of experience and specialist supervision, as the Squadron will largely be made up of inexperienced crews.*' Crews would undertake a number of 'ops' with 106 to gain initial operational experience before moving on to pathfinder training at Warboys in Cambridgeshire, on completion of which they would return for an additional 'op' with 106 before transferring to one of 5 Group's Pathfinder squadrons.

LACW Jean Danford had been posted with 97 Squadron, on its return to 5 Group, to Coningsby four months earlier and towards the end of September found that she was being posted again, this time to RAF

In the Middle of Nowhere - *The History of RAF Metheringham*

Jean Danford - MT driver (crew 'bus)

Barbara Allen - clerk, Orderly Room

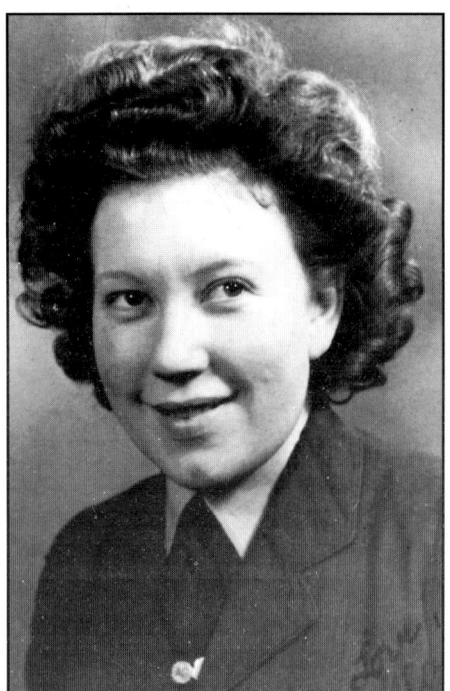

Gladys Marratt - clerk, Station Post Office

Anne Sheridan - MT driver (1690 BDTF)

Metheringham. She was a little surprised to find that the pilot with whom she shared the transport from Coningsby was being posted to fighter duties at what she understood was a bomber station, F/O Parlato, a New Zealander, was to join 1690 BDTF as a Hurricane pilot. Jean, an MT driver, on reporting for duty discovered that she was to be a crew-bus driver a job which, at her previous stations, had been the province of her male colleagues. With plenty of wide open spaces in which to practise and with guidance from another WAAF driver she quickly became accustomed to the size of the vehicle and familiar with the layout of the Station.

F/O Harvey Clarke, bomb aimer, arrived with his crew at Metheringham in mid September having just finished a weeks Lancaster familiarisation training at 5 Lancaster Finishing School, Syerston marking the completion of their bomber training which, until then, had been flown mainly on Wellingtons and Stirlings. Operational flying training continued at Metheringham until his pilot's 'second dickey' trip on 27th to Karlsruhe *'Our mid-upper gunner went with him as theirs was sick and then I got a call to replace a bomb aimer who had a cold. So off I went with F/O Tutton and his crew. I got an aiming point photograph through a hole in the cloud and I felt quite chuffed on return, especially when I saw that the skipper had got back too.'*

The cinema/theatre had by now received the long awaited and much more comfortable tiered seating and together with the newly installed stage lighting, the latter by a generous arrangement with 20th Century Fox and Rank, allowed the Station to proclaim this popular venue *'one of the best in the Command.'* Friday nights had usually been reserved for live shows in the theatre, films being shown for the remaining nights, however the increasing availability of travelling variety shows often resulted in the rescheduling of the weekly cinema programme. Cpl Ted Bullen, Clerk/GD, designed and painted posters advertising films being shown at the cinema, earning himself some extra money for his efforts, and also assisted regularly '..*Paddy (Cpl* Breen, from the Accounts Section) *was the cashier and I an "usherette". We also ran midnight showings for the girls from the NAAFI'* The Canadian Salvation Army show 'All Clear', staged on Thursday 12th October, featured a larger than average company, with forty artistes taking part, this show was voted a *' most stupendous entertainment'* the theatre being filled to capacity fifteen minutes before curtains up. As so many were unable to see the show the theatre was offered for a repeat performance but unfortunately the company had no free engagements.

Night bombing presented its own hazards for the crews irrespective of the fighters and flak encountered over the occupied countries. Individual

In the Middle of Nowhere - *The History of RAF Metheringham*

Station HQ and Accounts Section staff

Ted Bullen and Paddy Breen

aircraft flew at varying heights within the bombing force rarely seeing any other aircraft, except perhaps in the glow of fires over the target or when on 'ops' in the moon period, although their presence was often felt when an aircraft bucked in the slipstream of another. Fortunately collisions were infrequent although once over the target area the risk increased as did the likelihood of being hit by bombs released from aircraft at a higher altitude. S/Ldr Grindon found himself in such a position whilst attacking the port at Bremen on 6th/7th October. Incendiaries from another aircraft hit his port inner fuel tank, which drained completely within a few minutes, and, almost immediately after, the aircraft was hit by flak in the starboard centre tank. By using fuel from the centre tank until it was empty and by careful nursing of his engines he managed to reach the emergency landing ground at Woodbridge on the remaining fuel, landing without mishap.

Poor weather conditions were affecting 5 Group's operations during October and very often aircraft took off not knowing where they would land on return. Ten of 630 Squadron's Lancasters landed at Metheringham on the 20th, after a raid on Nuremburg, because of bad visibility at East Kirkby and five days later ten of 106's aircraft were diverted to Lossiemouth as fog covered almost all of England. Sixteen aircraft attacking submarine pens at Bergen, on the 28th/29th, found the whole of 5 Group's area covered by fog and diverted to airfields all over Yorkshire.

During the attack on Nuremburg which, whilst not a disaster for the bombing force as had been the previous attack in March, again had not been entirely successful. This time due to almost total cloud cover over the target and, with target markers being difficult to see, the attack was scattered. Very little nightfighter opposition had been encountered but for the first time members of the Squadron caught brief glimpses of a jet propelled fighter, type unknown, but which did not engage in combat.

Despite the wet and foggy weather airmen and women were at last able to move around the quarters and other sites without venturing into a sea of mud and attention had now turned to tree planting. Several hundred silver birch, fir and rhododendrons lined roadways and filled vacant plots of ground creating what the Station Commander called *'a garden city look'*. Throughout the summer months the squadrons within 54 Base had competed in the Inter Squadron Sports Competition, the prize being the Base Commander's Trophy. Every kind of indoor and outdoor sport had been played and, in a neck and neck finish with 83 Squadron, 106 clinched the Trophy by a mere two points in the final rounds of badminton and rifle shooting.

The WAAF's handicraft classes were becoming increasingly popular, even to the extent of being joined by airmen, particularly as attention turned to

54 BASE
INTER SQUADRON SPORTS PROGRAMME

AT CONINGSBY

Sgt's Mess Ground

14-30 hrs

making soft toys and other items ready for Christmas. When suitable material could be obtained from the suppliers, Dryad, dressmaking classes were also offered. Jean Danford recalls that their Nissen hut quarters, although made as homely as possible and given names such as 'Tree Tops', were still drab until the original depressing brown interior walls were redecorated with a more pleasing green. Jean worked a 24 hour shift starting at 8.00 in the morning. *'My day started by giving the 'bus a DI (Daily Inspection), then I went and parked outside the crew room until the crews were ready to be taken out to their aircraft for inspections. Not all of one crew would go out at the same time and so you would be back and forth all the time either taking or collecting someone. When off duty we spent part of the day sleeping then washing, ironing and the usual chores in the billet and perhaps in the evening go with friends to the pub in Martin or to some get together on the camp. One night a week was Domestic Night so you weren't allowed out unless on duty. Time was spent polishing your bed space, and that of the girls who were on duty, and in general giving the hut a good clean. Once that was finished we would have to go and clean the ablutions. When everything was done the Duty WAAF Officer and Sergeant would come and inspect our efforts, sometimes a kit inspection was thrown in as well.'*

WAAFs quarters ready for inspection

JB 663 'King of the Air' with it's groundcrew and their 'Chiefy' F/Sgt AV 'Tubby' Hallett, second left front row

Chapter 7
THE SECOND WINTER

Lancaster JB 663, 'King of the Air', one of a batch of 550 Mark IIIs built between June and December 1943, had been delivered to Metheringham on 18th November 1943 taking off on its first operation a little over a week later, an attack on Berlin on 26th/27th. Now, almost one year later on 4th/5th November 1944, it was about to take off on its one hundredth operation, an attack on the Dortmund-Ems canal near Ladbergen. This stretch of the canal had been successfully attacked in September when the banks had been damaged, draining the canal for several miles and leaving barges, taking coke from the Ruhr to steelworks at Brunswick and Osnabruck, high and dry seriously affecting steel production. The damage had now been repaired and 5 Group were to make a return visit. Once again a very accurate attack breached the banks in the same place draining the water. 'King of the Air' brought back its crew for this night, pilot F/O Day, safely as it had so many others. JB663 went on to complete one hundred and eleven 'ops' by the end of the war before being Struck off Charge and broken up at 15 MU Wroughton in October 1946.

Two nights later an attempt was made to drain the Mitteland Canal near Gravenhorst. Weather conditions were bad on the outward leg but cleared in the target area, however the 627 Squadron Mosquitoes had some difficulty locating the target and eventually only thirty one of the two hundred and thirty five Lancaster force released their bombs, the remainder being ordered to abandon the raid. The bombers met with considerable opposition over the target, crews reported Me109s, FW190s and jet aircraft, and ten Lancasters were lost including one from 106, that of F/O Neale's crew. Heavy rain back at Metheringham meant that only nine of the eighteen returning aircraft were able to land at base the rest being diverted to other airfields. After jettisoning some of its 1,000 pounders in the North Sea one of these found itself directed to Hethel, in Norfolk, home of the 389th

Martin village hall (right)

Bomb Group, USAAF. The crew were more than happy after being treated to a large breakfast of flapjacks, maple syrup and as many eggs as they could eat, then waiting until the 389th's Liberators had taken off for a daylight raid before returning to Metheringham.

The winter sporting fixtures resumed in earnest for a full programme of Inter Section competitions and, between squadrons for the Base Commander's Trophy. In the latter 106 got off to a good start beating 97 squadron 6-0 at table tennis. In practise for the Inter Section Competition the Station Armament soccer team played Ruskington Home Guard winning 3-1. A number of Station personnel attended a charity boxing match, arranged by the National Fire Service in Lincoln, to see their representative LAC Adamson, a South African, box well to beat Sgt. Rees of RAF Cranwell in the heavy weight competition.

Sgt W E (Bill) Winter's tour from Metheringham was completed largely over the winter of 1944/45 which *'..meant darkness from teatime onwards and, if not flying, the choice was between staying in the tin Nissen hut around the coke stove, drinking in the Sergeants Mess or down at the local pub in Martin village, always crowded with airmen, both aircrew and ground staff. I can still picture the one room pub, there were no beer pumps and no spirits. The landlord operated with a large white jug which he kept filling from barrels in the back room cellar, which necessitated going down a few steps out of the drinking room. Sometimes we called in at the village/church hall where dances were held and one could partake of various sandwiches of meat paste or dried egg. An abiding memory is that of a small rear gunner, from another crew, who was quite a jitterbug expert and entertained the audience with his antics. Other than that we had trips to Lincoln on a wooden seated 'bus which was the only means of transport apart from some lucky crews who clubbed together and managed to obtain an old banger. At one party in the Sergeants Mess the cook* managed to provide a concoction which he said was ice cream - quite a good attempt really!'

Although used to the many and frequent visitors, who came to inspect or report on every imaginable aspect of the Station's activities, there were still the occasional surprises as in the case of three Lieutenant Colonels of the Chinese Air Force who arrived in mid November. They spent three days looking into the workings of the Station HQ and the amenities available to Station personnel in preparation for a longer stay, early in the new year, when they planned to carry out a full study of administrative procedures. In keeping with the Station's record for being leaders in most things the Flying Control Section achieved first place in the quarterly 5 Group Flying Control Competition, whilst 1690 BDTF received a commendation from the AOC 5 Group for their *'excellent achievements since arriving at Metheringham'* and for *'.....their material contribution to the operational efficiency of the Group'*

Early November saw the responsibility for the Station's defence change once again as 2751 AA Squadron was replaced by 2763 AA Squadron RAF Regiment. An advance party travelled to Metheringham from its base at Portreath on the 6th followed on the 9th by the main party with the CO S/Ldr Mellor. This unit, with a strength of one hundred and forty three men, had just twelve days to settle in before receiving its first inspection by representatives of 54 Base and 5 Group.

Having returned, two weeks earlier, to the Dortmund-Ems canal draining it yet again the Squadron set out for the third time in three days, on 11th December, in an attempt to breach the Urft Dam close to the town of Heimbach. The allied front line was only some three miles to the west of the dam and the object of the attack was to flood the valley below the dam, whilst still in German occupation, rather than allow him to blow it up in front of the advancing allied army when he was finally forced to retreat. On the first visit 9/10ths cloud severely restricted bombing and little result was achieved, whilst the second attack was called off as the force crossed the Channel. Aircraft arriving over the target on this third attempt found cloud down to 5,000 ft so the controller ordered crews down below this level, although the area was soon obscured by smoke. Harvey Clarke recalls *'...we had to drop down to three thousand feet to get a clear view of the Dam and I got an aiming point photograph, because I knew how to reset my camera for the lower level. I saw my stick of bombs bursting all the way up the spill way.'* Despite the many hits seen on the dam it was not breached.

An indication of the heavy fighting taking place at this time to push the allied lines forward occurred when three hundred casualties arrived by air, directly from France, on 1st December with virtually no warning. Hurried arrangements provided temporary accommodation in the Station's Diversion Centre, normally reserved for crews on 'ops' or training flights diverted from other stations, until they could be transferred to hospital at Nocton Hall. Three days later two hundred and six wounded left via Metheringham for Renfrew, in nine C47s, on the first stage of their journey home.

Bill Winter, wireless operator with F/O Gray's crew, remembers that on one operation they were diverted to Kinloss due to bad weather. There they found another crew from Metheringham who had suffered engine problems and who were due to go on leave. The two pilots agreed to change aircraft and the other crew returned to base to take their leave. The engine problems took longer to rectify than anticipated. Bill recalls that the starter had been damaged, but the ground crew eventually managed to start the offending engine and they took off for a test flight. *'There was a nasty oil leak which curtailed our air test and down we came again.'* Consultation with the AVRO factory at Glasgow resulted, after some time, in engineers arriving with a new starter. *'We were idling away the time visiting Forres and also taking a train to Elgin where we discovered that the pubs shut at 9.30pm. It was all very light-hearted for us, without a change of clothes, no shaving gear until we borrowed some and, most importanty of course, a sub from the accounts section of RAF Kinloss! I suppose it wasn't worth flying us back down to Metheringham as someone would have had to fly back to retrieve the repaired Lanc. We were there ten days and by then should have been on leave ourselves, we arrived back at Metheringham on 23rd December and as a result had both Christmas and New Year at home on leave.'*

Since the early days of the War 106 Squadron had undertaken minelaying operations (gardening), then their Hampdens could only carry one mine (vegetable) whereas the Lancaster could carry up to six. A variety of mines were used, ranging from one thousand pounds to two thousand pounds, they were robust and reliable devices fitted with a drogue parachute to slow them down before entering the water. Prior to 1943 they had to be dropped from a height of between six hundred and eight hundred feet to ensure accurate delivery and to reduce entry shock. Improvements in mine design led to the release height being increased to three thousand feet in 1943, a height which was still within effective range of light flak, but by the end of the year had increased to fifteen thousand feet. Whereas the earlier 'ops' required pinpoint navigation and timed runs, for release points to be plotted on a map by the crews, by 1944 H2S radar developments meant that a photograph of the radar screen would provide the required information. It was important to accurately record details of mines laid as, on return to base, this information would be required by the Naval Armaments (or Liaison) Officer in order that he could transfer the details to Admiralty charts. A Bomber Command report of 1944 recorded *'.....a new technique which enables mines to be dropped accurately from high altitudes has been developed and put into operation. In conjunction with H2S and the Mark XIV bombsight it is now possible for mines to be laid successfully over heavily defended areas either visually or through 10/10ths cloud.'* 'Gardening' extended from north Norway down to the Spanish border, each area of the coastline being identified by a code named after a flower, fruit or vegetable, inland waterways and canals were also targeted. Although enemy opposition to these 'gardening' 'ops' had increased considerably by this stage in the War and included purpose built flakships anchored in known mining areas together with early warning radar stations, nevertheless 'gardening' was still looked on as an easy 'op' because most often the main attack, by the bomber force, for that night would be against mainland Europe and, apart from a little flak and the occasional fighter, the odds of survival were much higher. For 106 this theory appears to have been correct as the only aircraft to be lost from Metheringham whilst laying sea mines was ND682 which on 15th/16th December failed to return from 'gardening' in the south east Baltic (Spinach). Nightfighters had harried the bombers on the outward leg and over the Baltic attacking two other 106 Lancasters, causing damage to one, but F/O Barratt and his crew were not heard from again. The Baltic was used as a training area by the enemy's U-boats and operations there and in the Bay of Biscay, a U-boat transit area, incurred the highest percentage losses of aircraft during 'gardening' 'ops'.

When in operation FIDO proved a spectacular sight with sheets of flame and, initially, lots of smoke and the newsworthiness of this spectacle was probably the reason British Gaumont Pictures paid a visit to Metheringham. FIDO was lit during daylight hours on 20th December and remained in operation for an hour and twenty minutes while filming took place and a repeat performance the following day allowed the cameramen to complete their work. In the early hours of 22nd FIDO was in use yet again, this time to land operational aircraft returning from 'gardening' in the Kattegat, from attacking the oil refineries at Politz, and from a diversionary raid on Schneidermuhl. As well as those of 106 there were also aircraft from 189, 617, 97 and 83 Squadrons. Of the latter S/Ldr Hatcher had returned from Politz and, in attempting to land at Metheringham, crashed on the northern edge of the airfield, his Lancaster caught fire. All except the rear gunner were killed. P/O Ingmire escaped with a broken left arm, dislocated hip

APPENDIX 197 TO
OPERATIONS RECORD BOOK.
DECEMBER.1944.

REPORT ON ENTERTAINMENT FOR DECEMBER, 1944.

December was a notable month in the history of entertainment on the Station because the Station Dramatic Society put on its first play which was a great success, and, by the grace of E.N.S.A. we were placed on a circuit of "A" class shows.
 The prospects for the New Year are therefore promising E.N.S.A. will provide one "A" show per fortnight, and we have now an enthusiastic concert party which hopes to present an original show early in February.

SUMMARY OF DECEMBER ENTERTAINMENT.

1) STAGE SHOWS.

a) On Friday, 1st. December, the Station Dramatic Society presented Gerald Savory s comedy "GEORGE AND MARGARET". The play was produced by CORPORAL JORDAN and an excellent performance was given. A repeat performance was given on Saturday, 2nd. December.
b) On Friday, 8th. December, E.N.S.A. brought a lease lend show of the usual mixed variety type, but above the usual standard in entertainment value.
c) On Friday, 15th. December, a Canadian show the "W" Debs visited the station. This was an all female party, well dressed and at moments spectacular, but lacked the downright comedy flashes which one expects from these Canadian shows, probably due to the absence of males in the party.
d) On Friday, 22nd. December, E.N.S.A. brought an A category variety show called "Merry Whirls". There was a marked difference between this and the previous variety shows which we have had. It was lively and of uniformly good standard.

2) MUSICAL CONCERTS.

Two Sunday evening concerts of recorded music have been held during the month one on 17th. December and one on 24th. December. These were conducted by F/O. LEBITT.

3) CINEMA SHOWS.

 The Station Cinema has maintained a good standard of entertainment during the month. On Christmas afternoon a free showing was given of Abbot and Costello in Keep em Flying" an appropriate film for, such an occasion.

The following films have been shown:-
December, 2nd. 3rd. 4th. Carmen Miranda and Alice Fay in "THE GIRLS HE LEFT BEHIND".
 "   5th.6th. 7th.   Tyrone Power in "MARK OF ZORRO".
 "   9th.10th.11th. Lynn Bari and Akim Tamiroff in "THE BRIDGE OF SAN LUIS REY".
 "   12th.13th.14th. Dennis Morgan and Irene Manning in " DESERT SONG".
 "   16th.17th.18th. James Cagney in "JOHNNY VAGABOND".
 "   19th.20th.21st. George Sanders and Philip Dorn in "THE NIGHT IS ENDING".
 "   23rd.24th.25th. Michael O'Shea and Susan Hayward in "JACK LONDON".
 "   26th.27th.28th. Hedy Lamarr and William Powell in "HEAVENLY BODY".
 "   30th. 31st.   Anna Neagle and Richard Greene in "YELLOW CANARY".

4) DANCES.

 A very enjoyable all ranks dance was held on Christmas Night in the N.A.A.F.I. In addition two airmen's dances have been held during the month.

and burns to his face and scalp but was undoubtedly saved as a result of the rear turret being torn from the airframe. The RAF Regiment stood guard over the remains of the aircraft until its removal.

That evening the Station theatre provided the venue for the *'first of the A class shows'* offered by ENSA. *'A lively show entitled the "Merry Whirls" did much to liven the tedium of a dispersed station'*, the company being entertained in the Officers' Mess after the performance. The evening contributed to the festive spirits and with weather conditions hampering operations the Squadron was stood down allowing all the pre-planned activities to proceed. Christmas morning saw the Officers' and Sergeants' Messes field teams in a soccer cum rugby match, played in wet and murky conditions, during which several team members were lost in the fog. Fortunately injuries sustained in the rough and tumble were superficial and when the game was finally abandoned, the Sergeants' Mess claiming a win, the missing players were found in the Officers' Mess bar, to which the Sergeants were invited during the morning. *'A hilarious meal time was enjoyed by all 'other ranks' who were waited on in an almost professional manner by the officers and senior NCOs.'* The traditional Christmas dinner *'...of turkey washed down by copious quantities of good beer and cider'* was followed by a free film show in the Astra, filled to capacity, where it was noted that several people were sleeping off the effects of the excellent dinner. An all ranks dance in the NAAFI rounded off the second Christmas Day at Metheringham. For all those who had their families living nearby a party in the Officers' Mess for the children, on the 30th, gave Father Christmas, ably played by S/Ldr Taylor the Chief Technical Officer, an opportunity to distribute all the toys and presents made in the handicraft classes during the past few months. The children enjoyed food prepared by cooks from all the messes before joining in with the entertainment including a Punch and Judy show.

To round off the year a 'gardening' sortie in the Kattegat was followed by an attack on enemy armour and troops in the Bastogne area in support of the Americans although, because of cloud covering the target indicators, most of the Lancasters brought their bombs home. For their first operation in 1945 the Squadron revisited the Dortmund-Ems canal, at Ladbergen, which had again been repaired and once again left it drained.

Bill Winter had been delighted when Sergeant Harry Stunnel was posted to Metheringham, with F/O J Scott's crew, in early November 1944, both men had completed their training together and had become good friends. Sgt Ron Needle, rear gunner with F/O Scott's crew, remembers Harry walking into their billet not long after joining the Squadron and, for want of something to say, commented ' *Everyone seems flak happy around here.*' This drew an immediate response from one occupant of the billet who looked up from his game of monopoly and replied with some feeling ' *You'd be bloody flak happy if you'd had flak up your arse!*' Ron who was nineteen years of age attended a briefing at which the intended target was revealed as Berlin. *'Knowing the heavy losses incurred on previous raids to Berlin I did feel afraid, particularly when everyone else seemed to cheer at the news. Sometime later however we were called back to the briefing room to be told the raid was off, you should have heard the roar and clapping that greeted that statement.*' On their sixth 'op' from Metheringham F/O Scott's crew, in PB724, were subjected to six separate attacks by JU 88s on the run in to the target, the railway yards at Heilbronn, and were forced to jettison their bombs two miles south west of the target. Two nights later, on 6th December, they were again molested by JU88s before and after bombing the railway yards at Geissen although this time they managed to deliver their bombs accurately and achieved an 'Aiming Point' photograph. At the mouth of the River Gironde the town of Royan was still held by the Germans preventing the Allies using the port at Bordeaux and efforts by a large force of the French Resistance had so far failed to make any impression. Bomber Command had been requested to attack the town on the night of 4th/5th January to dislodge the enemy. *'At the briefing we were told to leave our identification lights on and that the Germans were only occupying a small area around Royan'* recalls Ron Needle *'It was supposed to be an easy target. However near the target I noticed what I thought were other Lancs to starboard. They were not Lancs but flak which soon became very concentrated. We were not hit but it did affect the flight of the aircraft, so much so that the bomb aimer was unable to drop his bombs on the first run. I think we all knew that we were experiencing our most dangerous raid. My heart dropped when Bob called out "dummy run", I knew we had to fly back on ourselves facing the barrage of guns on both sides of the estuary.*' He had good reason to recall the "flak happy" incident in the billet. *'On most of our raids we had to contend with enemy fighters and although afraid I was able to fire back, you couldn't fire back at flak.*' Almost ninety percent of the small town had been destroyed, but unknown to Bomber Command there were still about two thousand French civilians in the town, between five hundred and eight hundred of whom were killed. A truce was called to search for survivors in the ruins. The Germans had suffered only light casualties and continued to hold out until the middle of April.

Three nights later as Bill Winter pulled on his flying gear he chatted with Harry Stunnel who had the locker next to his, Bill recalls ' *He remarked* that he had a funny feeling about that night's trip, which was to Munich. I tried to reassure him that we all felt like that at times but he was insistent that the premonition was strong and that something would go wrong that night.' Sixteen aircraft took off to attack the town centre and industrial areas. Harry remembers '*We had bombed the target from 20,000ft and, as we were flying dead straight and level on the thirty second duration photographic run, another aircraft, a Lancaster, bore down upon us from an oblique high angle flicked our wing tip and turned us upside down.*' He and the rest of the crew were powerless to move, due to the extreme G forces, and unable to bale out as the Lancaster went into a steep dive. '*But then, after an eternity and after having fallen to a mere 2,000ft. the pilot and engineer between them somehow righted our damaged aircraft. It was one of the severest winters in living memory. Europe had been snowbound for about six weeks and we flew on through the night at low level into the teeth of a raging snow blizzard. We had jettisoned the underside front escape hatch for the abandon aircraft command, but we kept flying and crossed over Strasbourg into the Lorraine province of France.*' The blast of ice cold air through the open hatch caused the inside of the aircraft to ice over and they all shivered uncontrollably '*Then in the most deplorable conditions we ran into high ground near a village between Nancy and Metz. We ploughed into a dense forest on top of a range of hills and caught fire. Five crew members, including the pilot, were instantly killed by the impact. Above my head, in the wireless operator's compartment, the perspex astrodome melted and I climbed out of the resultant hole.*' His clothing on fire he had to roll in the snow to put out the flames. Unsure of their position, with no sign of any houses nearby and unable to move far because of their injuries and the blizzard, they took what shelter they could from the snow and biting wind. As daylight came there seemed to be little hope of help being at hand but then the sound of the Angelus could be heard from a distant church bell. After spending ten hours on the hillside Harry staggered into the small village of Meligny le Grand where he was taken in and cared for by Madame Giroux.

Meanwhile the bellringer, Andre Fromont, joined a search party to locate the crash site. They found Ron barely conscious and scarcely able to move. Harry suffered multiple third degree burns to both legs, whilst Ron sustained severe damage to one leg and internal injuries, both men also suffering from frostbite. They received medical care from the local doctor and the villagers before being taken to the 50th US Hospital at Commercy west of Nancy.

J A Wymark, 106 Squadron's Navigation Officer, flew regularly with

No. 106 Squadron,
Royal Air Force,
Metheringham,
Lincoln.
9th January 1945.

Dear Mr Stunell,

    I am writing to give all the details I have of the circumstances in which your son, Sergeant Henry Stunell, has been injured.

    On the night of 7/8th January 1945, my Squadron took part in the heavy and successful attack on Munich and your son was the wireless operator of one of the aircraft detailed for the raid. The aircraft did not return to Base at the scheduled time and after the petrol endurance limit had expired, I had no alternative but to assume it as lost, and I notified you accordingly.

    On Monday afternoon I received a message to the effect that the aircraft had crashed in France and that five members of the crew had lost their lives and the remaining two, including your son, had been injured. I telegraphed this news to you immediately.

    This morning I have been given further information. The reasons are not yet known, but the aircraft when on the homeward journey, crashed at Meligny-le-Grand, south west of Commercy, which is about thirty miles from Nancy.

    Your son has been admitted to the 50th General U.S. Hospital suffering from burns - the extent of which I do not yet know - but his general condition was satisfactory. The Hospital is presumably near Commercy and information may not be available as readily as one would wish but you may rest assured that that you will be kept informed of news of the condition of your son as soon as it is received.

    If there is any way in which I can be of assistance please do not hesitate to write and I will do my best to help you.

Yours sincerely,

W. W. J. Stevens W/Cdr.

Wing Commander, Commanding,
No. 106 Squadron, R.A.F.

Mr. H. J. STUNELL,
18, Carlton Place,

In the Middle of Nowhere - *The History of RAF Metheringham*

Squadron Leader Barden, B Fight Commander, and recounts a raid on the synthetic oil plant at Politz, near Stettin, on 13th/14th January. 'We took off at 16.30 with the usual band of Station personnel to wave us off in the twilight. Our route took us over the northern tip of Denmark, close to Copenhagen, to the Kattegat and close enough to Sweden to see the lights of Malmo. 106 Squadron was a back-up squadron to Pathfinders from Coningsby and Woodhall Spa. The Master Bomber had marked the target with flares in spite of poor visibility, and we were instructed to back up the marker flares and then go in and release our bombs. Flak was intense and accurate enough for us to hear the burst of shells over the engine noise. We set course over the Baltic for home on much the same route as we came. Our starboard outer engine was giving trouble, probably hit with flak shell fragments. Arthur Barden decided to feather the propeller and shut off the engine. We now had some five hours flying time to Lincolnshire, and it would make petrol consumption critical with increased power on three engines if we were to maintain height and speed. The engineer soon worked out that we would exhaust our fuel over the North Sea. Arthur therefore decided to put the aircraft in a slow descent from thirteen thousand feet until we reached two thousand feet. In the meantime I worked out a shorter course to base across the southern part of Denmark. Our danger was being picked up by German radar. However, we were at two thousand feet over Denmark which made radar detection less likely. In the meantime, I had kept a note of a course to the Swedish coast in case we lost another engine. Arthur found that we could maintain two thousand feet at about one hundred and thirty miles per hour instead of our usual one hundred and fifty five. We were below the cloud level but we could see the coastline of Denmark and we were now in range of our own radar. The engineer was now busy working out the petrol consumption on the three engines as best he could from the petrol gauges. He also had the job of using fuel tanks to give the best handling of the aircraft. He decided that we could make base with a few gallons to spare, the alternative would have been to make the marginally shorter course to Norfolk. However, this would have meant breaking radio silence. The Germans had a habit of picking up 'lame ducks' on radio and sending a night fighter to finish them off. All went well, except that we were now nearly an hour behind our scheduled time. We could hear on the radio the rest of the Squadron getting permission to land when we were way out over the North Sea. As soon as we crossed the Lincolnshire coast, we broke silence, and reported our plight. What a relieved voice we heard from Wing Commander Stevens, who was Duty Officer at base. He immediately established that there were no 'bandits' in the area. There was a light westerly wind down the main runway, so that we were able to come straight in without circling, which is difficult on three engines.

S/Ldr Arthur Barden and crew

Wheels came down OK, flaps seemed to be alright, Arthur was prepared also should a tyre have been damaged. We landed safely at 03.10. Breakfast of bacon, eggs and fried potatoes went down very well.'

    Meanwhile Sgt McPhail, who had been shot down and captured on 24th June the previous year, escaped with five other prisoners and with the help of the Polish resistance, from Stalag Luft 7 near Kluczbork in Poland eventually making contact with the advancing Russians. It took a further two months however before he finally reached home via Odessa and Port Said

    Snow had been falling on and off since the 4th at Metheringham and only by concerted effort were the runways kept clear. On several days the snow ploughs were in action continuously and although there was a slight thaw mid month the snow returned with a vengeance culminating in a blizzard on 30th when it fell to a depth of almost ten inches. The wireless and newspapers reported that this had been the coldest January for eighty years a fact concurred with by the WAAFs who had won the "longest icicle" competition with one of *'three feet five inches'* found on their Quarters site picket post. Surprisingly there had been few problems with the water supply, however the Land Army girls from Martin Manor did have to bring buckets on a pony and trap to the Airmen's Mess to collect water. Jean Danford had been detailed to drive a Corporal from the Station Post Office into Lincoln and back ' There was heavy snow and the roads were like an ice rink and he kept trying to grab the handbrake. On the return journey we had just got to the top of a hill where there was a large verge before some houses. All of a sudden he grabbed the handbrake and the van spun like a top, we just missed a telegraph pole and the snow on the verge stopped us. On the way back he heard some home truths from me and I refused to take him any further than the MT section. Someone else took him where he wanted to go and they ended up in a ditch, the Corporal received a nasty cut on his forehead, whether that taught him a lesson I don't know.'

The Chinese delegation returned in mid January and spent a week with the Station Admin. Officer, S/Ldr Whattam, gathering information about the various administrative procedures in place on a typical RAF Station. They were found to be particularly interested in personnel matters and various quarters were inspected during their visit drawing favourable comment, in particular the WAAFs 'bedrooms' being described as 'beautiful'.

Little damage had been caused to Siegen on the 1st/2nd February, most of the bombs falling onto open countryside near the town. As he prepared for the return leg F/O Gray's Lancaster was hit in both port engines, one

F/O WE Hamilton lends a hand with snow clearing

caught fire. He managed to reach the former Luftwaffe airfield at Juvincourt, in France, making a forced landing which left the bomber half a mile past the end of the runway in a boggy field. Bill Winter remembers 'Several damaged aircraft, strafed by Allied fighters, littered the place and there were heaps of German bombs still lying about showing evidence of a hasty retreat. The field was used by American fighters by day and as an emergency landing ground for Bomber Command by night. The Americans treated us very well

In the Middle of Nowhere - *The History of RAF Metheringham*

even providing fresh grapefruit, a novelty to us, they even unearthed some tea! Later that morning a stroll down to the village revealed evidence of quite a land battle with many damaged buildings, this was our first-hand sight of the war. The village church had survived and, on entering, we found the floor newly washed and strewn with reeds - quite a peaceful haven in the middle of the war torn village.' Venturing into Rheims he came across a large compound near the railway station being used as a temporary prisoner of war camp for captured enemy soldiers. *'As we watched a large contingent of young German soldiers was being shepherded along the street, towards the compound, by American soldiers. They had only recently been captured and looked very dispirited, unkempt, unshaven and not at all like the so called glorious Wehrmacht portrayed by Goebells in his propaganda. When they saw us and recognised our RAF uniforms they edged away to the other side of the road.'* Leaving their own aircraft at Juvincourt for repairs F/O Gray and crew returned to Metheringham in a 44 Squadron Lancaster, itself having taken advantage of the emergency airfield a few days earlier. On the advice of the ground crew though they flew this patched up aircraft with the undercarriage down.

A welcome 'cuppa' and a chance for a short break courtesy of the YMCA van

Chapter 8
ANTICIPATION.....

Once again responsibility for the Station's defences changed as 2763 AA Squadron departed for RAF Wyton to be replaced by 2832 AA Squadron, from RAF Bourn, commanded by S/Ldr R Bell. Although 2763 took their small arms with them the larger calibre Hispano anti aircraft guns were handed over to the incoming unit. The new arrivals scarcely had time to settle in before being visited by defence advisers from HQ 5 Group ensuring that there would be no slackening in reaction to possible enemy intruders. However by early March the strength of 2832 would begin to be depleted as men were transferred to the army, the need for airfield defence by then being almost unnecessary.

John Woodrow, having completed sixty three 'ops' as an air gunner with 57 Squadron at East Kirkby, remustered as a Warrant Officer MT driver at the end of 1944. Initially posted to Coningsby, upon arrival he was given the choice of the three stations within 54 Base to take up his duties. He chose Metheringham as, being the furthest from Coningsby a prewar station, he expected there would be less discipline although it might not have been so cold in the quarters at Coningsby that winter as it was at Metheringham. He recalls taking an old Crossley to a laundry at Grimsby once a week, upon its return the recipients of the freshly laundered washing would find messages from the laundry girls. His uncle worked for a fish wholesaler in Grimsby and he would often return with a box of fish to be sold on the Station. There being no dinghy training tank at Metheringham John made frequent trips to South Park School in Lincoln to allow the aircrews to get their dinghies wet in the school swimming pool as a change from dinghy drill next to an aircraft at dispersal.

As weather conditions during January had precluded operations or training flying during the latter part of the month an improvement in February allowed some of the lost time to be made up. 1690 BDTF wasted no time in resuming fighter evasion training for the Lancaster crews and on 10th February a Hurricane undertook a routine series of mock attacks on a Lancaster from nearby RAF Spilsby. Having completed the exercise, and with an R/T malfunction, the two aircraft both broke to starboard at seven thousand feet over Wainfleet and collided. The Hurricane pilot baled out and landed safely his aircraft crashing near Wainfleet. Four members of the Lancaster's crew baled out although the pilot, after overshooting on his first attempt, successfully landed the aircraft at its base. Three of those baling out landed without injury whilst the body of the fourth was found several days later apparently having slipped through his parachute harness. Two days after the incident the 1690 pilot, complaining of back pains, was found to have a fractured vertebra.

A fourth attack on the Dortmund - Ems canal had met without success as almost all of the half hour delay bombs fell in surrounding fields causing no damage to the canal banks.

The Eastern Front had by now reached the very borders of Germany and a number of targets had been identified, in eastern Germany, as likely to cause maximum disruption to an already hard pressed enemy. Large scale raids on these targets, being communication and supply centres and also crowded with refugees fleeing from the advancing Russians, would cause maximum confusion and seriously hamper any reinforcements reaching the Eastern Front and thus help the Russian allies, who had requested that such attacks be made. On the night of 13th/14th February Bomber Command was to attack one of these selected targets, Dresden. 5 Group led the first wave of the attack with 106's crews reporting a target obscured by 10/10ths cloud to a height of 6,000ft. They bombed using the glow on the clouds from the target markers and although the results appeared good they were only moderately successful. The second wave, three hours later, found that the cloud had dispersed and released their HE and incendiary bombs with great accuracy, creating a firestorm which burned out large areas of the city, killing an estimated fifty thousand people.

For the remainder of the month attention turned to shipping targets with attacks on ports together with the regular 'gardening 'sorties. On a raid to Horten, Oslo Fjord, to attack a possible U-boat base and shipping, F/O Hamilton experienced problems with one engine and, having nursed it in order to reach bombing height, decided to shut it down. Harvey Clarke, his bomb aimer, discreetly suggested to their navigator that they should cut out the dog-leg on the outward route otherwise *'..we would be a bit late on target, which would be dicey with fighters about. We caught up the time and bombed with the rest and started for home. Soon after leaving the coast we* dropped down to sea level and arrived home thirty minutes later than the others.'

In the early hours of 4th March Jean Danford sat in her crew bus on a dispersal awaiting the return of five aircraft from a 'gardening' sortie to Oslo Fjord. *'I had just seen the first one coming in to land when all the lights went out and the Station was in darkness, by then the Lancaster had lifted off again and I had no idea what was going on.'* Unbeknown to Jean the five aircraft had been told to 'Scram', as enemy intruders had been reported in the area, and they diverted to Bittesville. *'I waited a while and then decided to go back to the crew room to find out what was going on. I had just crossed one of the runways when I heard a 'plane which seemed to be too fast for a bomber. Immediately there was the sound of rapid gunfire and as I looked back I saw the flash on the perimeter track just a few yards behind as the bullets hit the ground. I flew round the perimeter track to the crew room, parked the 'bus, and dashed inside. There was a mass of people there, a WAAF officer told me that enemy aircraft had been waiting for our bombers to return, a warning had been tannoyed all over the camp but I hadn't heard it. After a cup of tea I watched, with the others, from the doorway, there was a right old battle going on as the gunners were firing at the fighters which in turn were firing back, it seemed to go on for ages.'* Thanks to the timely warning the enemy had not caught any of 106's returning Lancasters, the RAF Regiment had put up a spirited defensive fire and, although not claiming any intruders shot down, they had prevented any damage or casualties being inflicted. The all clear was finally given two hours after Jean had first seen the lights go out.

Sgt W (Bill) Williams arrived at Metheringham on 20th February, his twentieth birthday. He and the rest of his crew captained by F/O B Gordon had already volunteered, and been accepted, for Pathfinder duties and after training at Warboys during March they would transfer to 97 Squadron at Coningsby early in April, firstly they would need to gain operational experience. Their first 'op' on 6th March took them to the small Baltic port of Sassnitz, a nine and a quarter hours round trip from Metheringham. Take off was scheduled for 1830 hours and, after lunch, having recently acquired a large car F/O Gordon decided to take his crew for a ride. Along one of the typically straight fen roads the car came to a halt and refused to restart, the crew climbed out and began to push. By now they were beginning to panic as it was approaching briefing time and the car still refused to start. Eventually, and after pushing it for a considerable distance, the engine fired, quickly jumping back in they made it back to the Station with fifteen minutes to spare. A week later they were on their fifth 'op', the target a synthetic oil refinery at Lutzkendorf. Thick fog at Metheringham meant a di-

THE LANCASTRIAN DANCE ORCHESTRA

Leader: Stan Green - - Tenor Clarinet
Stan Sharman - - Alto Clarinet
Jock Wilson - - Tenor Violin
"Toni" - - - Piano
John Keatley - - - Drums

Stage Manager - - - Donald Jordan
Stage Electrician - - - Arthur Parr
Stage Carpenter - - - Harry Brown
Settings and Paints - - - Jimmy Madden
Accompanist and Orchestra Arrangements - "Toni"
Make-Up Artist - - - Phil Dresman
Dresser - - - - Philippa Taylor
Chorology - - - - Mary Angus

VOTE OF THANKS.

To The Station Commander and all Officers i/c Sections for their unstinted co-operation during the production of this Revue.

To The Nottingham Theatrical Supply for their kind assistance.

R.A.F., METHERINGHAM

By kind permission of G/Capt. M. L. Heath

The Rev. ERIC W. ROBOTHAM

presents

"AS YOU LIKE IT"

A MODERN REVUE

Produced by PHIL DRESMAN

AS YOU LIKE IT

COMPERED BY "DOC" JOYCE

1. OVERTURE

2. "IN THE GROOVE"
   Billy Robotham, Phil Dresman, Carol Macfarlane and cast.

3. "THE NEWS"
   Chris Foscolo, Diane Sowerby, Alan Mack, Phil Dresman.

4. "BOTHER"
   Jock Wilson and Alan Mack.

5. "WHEN DAY IS DONE"
   Ron Terry, Queenie Newton, Wally Wale, Bob MacDonald, Diane Sowerby, Freddie Palmer, Bill Dartford, Mary Angus, Carol Macfarlane, Trixy Hector, Betty Swindells, Mary Hines, Caroud Balfour.

6. "YOU CAN'T HELP LAUGHING"
   Phil Dresman.

7. "GREASE LIGHTNING"
   Jimmy "Omar" Madden

8. "SOMETHING DIFFERENT"
   Diane Sowerby, Jock Wilson, Betty Swindells, Mary Angus, Carol Macfarlane, Trixy Hector, Mary Hines, "Toni," Jimmy Madden, Ron Terry, Caroud Balfour, Chris Foscolo, Phil Dresman.

9. "SOMETHING NEW"
   Billy Robotham, Betty Swindells, Jock Wilson, Alan Mack, Phil Dresman, Betty Williams.

10. "ON A STRING"
    Arthur Pickles

11. "TONI" and FOSCOLO.

12. "MORE BOTHER"
    Philippa Taylor and Phil Dresman.

12a. "ONE HUNDRED AND SIX CLUB"
    Doreen Reynolds, Betty Williams, Gordon Orr, Queenie Newton, Ron Terry, Bill Dartford, Mary Angus, Carol, Trixy, Betty, Mary Hines, and full cast.

Betty Swindells

Carol Macfarlane

Four members of the cast of 'As You Like It'

Queenie Newton

Rev Eric W (Billy) Robotham

version to Silverstone which, by the time they arrived, was also fog bound, after overshooting twice F/O Gordon managed to put the aircraft down with a bump which almost had them airborne again.

F/O Richardson also found himself diverted to Silverstone on return from the same target. In contact with flying control he eventually saw the airfield lights and made his approach and was instructed to report to the tower on landing. Taxiing off the runway he duly reported to the control tower to be greeted by Americans having inadvertently landed at Molesworth, home to the Flying Fortresses of the 303rd Bomb Group, USAAF. F/Sgt. A D (Sandy) Wilson, wireless operator, remembers *'They made us very welcome and gave us coffee, the best I've ever tasted, before insisting on showing us round their B17s. I was surprised at the small bomb load that they could carry and at the small size of the bombs.'* One Lancaster, LL948, with F/O E Barrow's crew aboard failed to return from Lutzkendorf. This was the last operational loss from Metheringham.

Prior to this operation all Squadron members had gathered in front of a Lancaster, close to the Repair and Inspection hangar, for the official Squadron photograph and whilst awaiting the photographer they witnessed the arrival of four C-47s from France. Because of poor visibility, due to fog, FIDO was lit to aid their landing and, sometime later, they evacuated one hundred stretcher cases from Nocton Hall to Prestwick taking off again using FIDO.

On 11th March another incident occurred involving a 1690 BDTF Hurricane. Airborne over Metheringham at 2030 hours Hurricane PZ740 and a 463 Squadron Lancaster LM130 " Nick the Nazi Neutraliser", from Waddington, collided during a training exercise. The two aircraft crashed close to the airfield, both crews being killed. The Hurricane pilot, F/O Parlato, who had travelled to Metheringham from Coningsby with Jean Danford, had been with the Flight less than six months.

In support of the Rhine crossing 106 took part, on 23rd/24th, in an attack on Wesel which was captured by British Commandos soon after the bombers departed and before the defenders had time to recover. As a result of the attack casualties suffered by the Allied Forces were very light. Messages of thanks were received from Field Marshall Montgomery and from General Dempsey of the Commandos. Returning from this attack F/O Richardson's Lancaster was flying at 10,000ft when an object smashed through the cockpit windscreen and hit him in the face. With the pilot blinded the flight engineer instinctively pulled back the control column to maintain level flight and the bomb aimer, who had received flying training, took over. 'Sandy' Wilson finding that his pilot had perspex splinters in his eyes and a gash on his chin did his best to make him comfortable, but made no attempt to remove the splinters, this required medical expertise. The offending object was passed to him for identification. He carefully examined the remains of a bird, about the size of a fist, with a long beak, and recognising it as a snipe, placed it carefully on one side to be presented as evidence of the incident. Meanwhile the navigator decided that they should make for Manston and, although flying control there informed them that they should bale out, the crew declined because of the difficulties this would present to the pilot. F/O Richardson was helped back into his seat and, with help from the flight engineer and bomb aimer, landed the bomber by 'feel'. Although a slightly heavy landing, dropping in from twenty five feet, under the circumstances it was quite an achievement. F/O Richardson returned to operational flying on 30 April fortunately having suffered no damage to his eyesight.

The Rhine offensive and continuing successes of the Allied Forces created an air of expectancy within the minds of the general public and service personnel - how soon will it end?

Left to Right: F/Sgt Venables, F/Sgt Trinder, F/Sgt Wilson, F/Sgt Lovett, F/Lt Huggett, F/Sgt Breeze and F/O Richardson

Chapter 9
VICTORY IN EUROPE

A Halifax from 1663 Conversion Unit at Rufforth called up flying control at Metheringham shortly before midnight on 2nd April experiencing undercarriage trouble, low brake pressure and an overheating engine, and requested an emergency landing. The pilot having been instructed to use the emergency air supply to lower the undercarriage and then to land immediately, persisted in trying to make a belly landing although the undercarriage, when Flying Control finally persuaded him to use it, did prove serviceable. The whole crew was found to be French.

Taking off at around 1800 hours on 7th April nine aircraft from 106 were to precede the Pathfinders and drop 'window' to provide cover for them and the rest of the force attacking an oil installation at Molbis. This was not a popular idea with the Squadron since it meant flying ahead of the main force, dropping 'window' and then going round again for the bombing run once the target had been marked by the following Pathfinders. The Squadron CO, W/Cdr Levis, had returned for the bombing run when his aircraft was 'coned' by searchlights. Immediately the 'flak' opened up and at the same time a nightfighter prepared to attack. Being on the bombing run the pilot could not take evasive action and the gunners did not see the fighter until it closed in. Immediately the bombs were released W/Cdr Levis began a 'corkscrew' manoeuvre as cannon shells hit the Lancaster and the gunners returned fire. The single attack had damaged the hydraulic system putting the rear turret out of action, the bomb doors would not close and a fuel tank was holed, with the loss of about 200 gallons of fuel. The Lancaster was almost defenceless, one of the mid-upper guns having jammed but, by a piece of good fortune, the searchlights went out almost immediately and the fighter did not pursue its attack. The bomb aimer, Sgt. Fred Girkin, recalls '.. *seeing a lot of colourful lights heading straight for my face as I lay over the bomb sight. The mid-upper gunner reported that he was*

At rear (left to right) George Atkinson rear gunner, Fred Girkin bomb aimer, Dave Inch mid-upper gunner, George Clift wireless operator
Front (left to right) F/O Adshead flight engineer, Wing Commander Leslie Levis pilot and John Rogers navigator

hurt, broken perspex had cut his neck, and the engineer reported to the skipper that one, possibly two, engines were damaged.' Although he was reasonably sure that the bombs were released on target the aircraft was in the middle of a 'corkscrew' when the camera took the aiming point photograph and, despite protestations on return to base, Intelligence credited them with a considerable error. Coaxing U-Uncle homeward it became evident that there was not enough fuel to reach Metheringham, so the navigator suggested diverting to Wing where the crew had completed their training. Upon landing the Lancaster swung wildly off the runway and, leaving it where it came to rest, they removed their equipment to the control tower before being allocated an empty hut to sleep in. Sleep was difficult because the hut was in the process of being redecorated and smelled strongly of 'distemper'. Daylight revealed the full extent of the damage to U-Uncle, cannon shells had punched holes in two propeller blades on the starboard inner engine, damaged the starboard wheel and several shells had penetrated the bomb bay. Repairs would take some time so an aircraft flew down to Wing to ferry W/Cdr Levis and the rest of the crew back to Metheringham.

Returning from an attack on Lutzkendorf the following night F/O Hamilton's crew were diverted, with the rest of the Squadron's aircraft, to RAF

Long Marston due to bad weather over Metheringham. On their return to base the next day Harvey Clarke recalls *'We were taxiing round the perimeter track to our dispersal and we had to pass the Squadron offices and outside was the Wing Commander and some of the other bods who all waved to us as we passed. We waved back and I said its nice to know that you were wanted back, so to our dispersal and our happy ground crew. Around came the crew 'bus and we went back to the debriefing room.'* There they were greeted with the news that their tour had been shortened and as a result they had just completed their last 'op'. *'We were saved from that last trip jitters. Now we knew what all the waving was about and found out later that our ground crew and the WAAF bus driver had been sworn to secrecy not to let us know so that the Wing Commander could do his stuff when we got in. So it meant leave and postings afterwards, three of us from London were able to cadge a lift to Northolt four days later in an Anson. When we got back to camp nine days later I was the only one to stay with the Squadron. You don't think the Wing Commander was going to start looking for a new Bombing Leader and a new Messing Officer do you?'*

The Inspector General of the WAAF, Group Officer McLeod paid a visit, in mid April, to inspect the WAAF site and the amenities, she expressed *'...very great appreciation of the conditions under which the WAAFs were serving'* and was *'delighted with the sleeping quarters'*. The day after her visit officers from HQ 5 Group arrived to judge the WAAF quarters and amenities for the second round of the Sunderland Cup. Metheringham had been judged to have the best facilities in 54 Base and was one of four chosen from all of the 5 Group Stations and from which one had now to be selected to represent the Group in the competition to find the best in Bomber Command. The WAAFs were disappointed to lose out to Bardney but nevertheless, in the spirit of the competition, gladly gave advice when WAAF officers arrived from Bardney to gain a few ideas to improve their own chances in the competition.

On the night of 16th April fourteen aircraft were detailed to attack the railway yards at Pilsen. The twelfth aircraft, NG 414, lined up to take off and the gathered ground staff waved as it accelerated away down the runway. As they watched it gather speed they saw to their horror the Lancaster career off the runway, as it did so the undercarriage collapsed after striking the FIDO installation and the aircraft ground to a halt. Fortunately the crew were unhurt and quickly vacated the aircraft as fire broke out, the rear gunner's parachute was found two hundred yards away which, bearing in mind that the seat type pack would have been banging against the backs of his legs, was quite an achievement. He was later reported to have completed a lap of the perimeter track and overtaken the fire tender! W/Cdr Levis, who had joined the ground staff to see the aircraft off, ordered the remaining two aircraft, waiting to take off, back to their dispersals. Those fighting the fire were then ordered to withdraw as there was a very real danger of the load of 500 pounders and a 'cookie' going off along with the thousands of rounds of ammunition. 'Sandy' Wilson, not on 'ops' that night recalls being detailed to go into Martin to warn villagers of the possibility of an explosion and to suggest that windows were opened to reduce damage, this he did after quickly donning his greatcoat, over his pyjamas, and pulling on his boots. A navigator recalls *'I was not on 'ops' that night so I was in bed in a Nissen hut on the Martin road. Like the others in the room I was not asleep, but listening to the aircraft taking off, following each aircraft down the runway in my mind. I heard one aircraft's engines throttle back and the squeal of tyres as the pilot tried to stop it. I waited for a dramatic bang but nothing happened, I thought of the FIDO tanks with a reputed half a million gallons of petrol .We opened the door and saw flames over the rising ground between us and the airfield and debated whether to go over or stay where we were, deciding that we would be summoned over the tannoy if we were needed. We could have used the air raid shelters but they were so uncomfortable, we went back to bed having decided that the iron sheeting of the Nissen hut would be sufficient protection against flying debris. I understand that the violence of the crash scattered the bombs around and that the NCO in charge of the fire crew managed to get them to roll the 'cookie' away from the fire.'* The aircraft burned for some time, then exploded lifting tiles off the roof and breaking windows at Rosie Harrad's house only two or three hundred yards away from where the Lancaster came to rest. Thankfully the 'cookie' did not explode and all the bombs were made safe and removed the following morning.

Although unbeknown to the crews at the time an attack by sixteen of the Squadron's aircraft on an oil storage installation at Tonsberg, with two others mining in Oslo Fjord (Horten), on the 25th/26th April proved to be the Squadron's final offensive operation of the war.

On 30th April Hitler committed suicide in his bunker in Berlin and four days later German Officers signed a surrender document, in Field Marshall Montgomery's headquarters on Luneberg Heath, on behalf of all German forces in northwest Germany, Denmark and Holland. That same day seventeen 106 aircraft joined in on Operation Exodus, flying initially to Juvincourt and then to Rheine, to repatriate liberated British prisoners of war. Sgt. Fred Girkin remembers *' How frightening the hastily filled bomb craters at Rheine runway were. The skip made me lie in the nose of the aircraft as we landed, a practise normally taboo, so that I could help him avoid the worst of*

In the Middle of Nowhere - *The History of RAF Metheringham*

the pot holes. The anxious faces of the ex POWs looking up into my position in the aircraft's nose, a Flight Lieutenant, shot down in '41, in his best blue, rank rings tattered and held in place by just an odd strand of cotton.' A navigator on one of these flights recalls *' One of the Squadron's aircraft lost power in one engine while taking off with a load of passengers, it swung off the runway and came to grief in a bomb crater. I believe it narrowly avoided exploding a land mine* (which still littered the airfield). *Luckily there were no casualties. The flights must have been extremely uncomfortable for the passengers, their seats were merely numbers painted on top of the bomb bay and any other available space. Three had been allocated to my bench and I had to move one off the end so that I could get at the navigation table. It was a bit embarrassing trying to work with an interested audience at either elbow! Some were aircrew and obviously quite interested in the latest equipment'.*

For weeks everyone had been expecting the war to end at any day and plans had long been made for the celebrations. Finally on 7th May General Eisenhower accepted the unconditional surrender of all German forces on all fronts to be effective from 00.01 on 9th May. On the morning of 8th May, VE Day, the Station Commander announced the cessation of hostilities over the tannoy, all personnel not on essential duties were ordered to stand down and await instructions. Soon everyone was helping to prepare

'Ruff's Airlines' took part in Operation Exodus in May 1945, F/Lt Ruff and crew with their ground crew

WAAF Sergeants pose outside The Sarjery prior to attending a victory parade in Lincoln to mark VE Day

for the planned celebration dance. The Repair and Inspection hangar was emptied and the floor cleaned, an area in the centre was roped off to act as a dance floor and bundles of 'window' opened and the foil strips hung from the roof beams as decorations. The various messes spent much of the day preparing food, 'Sandy' Wilson recalls helping the catering staff prepare sandwiches *'the butter was heated slightly then put onto the bread with a brush similar to a shaving brush.'* Each mess set up a bar, local breweries had already been approached for additional supplies of beer, and wooden tables set out on which to lay out the large quantities of food being prepared. Locals from the surrounding villages were invited and the Station dance band provided the music as everyone danced the night away pausing only to enjoy the food and drink. For some the celebrations were spoiled by the announcement that they were required to fly the next morning, however they didn't object too much, as they went off to their billets, when they learned they would be repatriating more POWs. By midnight 'Sandy' was

54 Base produced this commemorative picture for VE Day

putting sweets and blankets into the Lancasters for the POWs as the ground crews prepared fifteen aircraft for an 0800 takeoff. Over the following week one thousand four hundred and ninety eight POWs, twenty four in each Lancaster, were repatriated, the majority to Dunsfold, and others to Westcott although the Station ORB records one civilian (believed to be female) being flown from Rheine to Metheringham, with no further explanation.

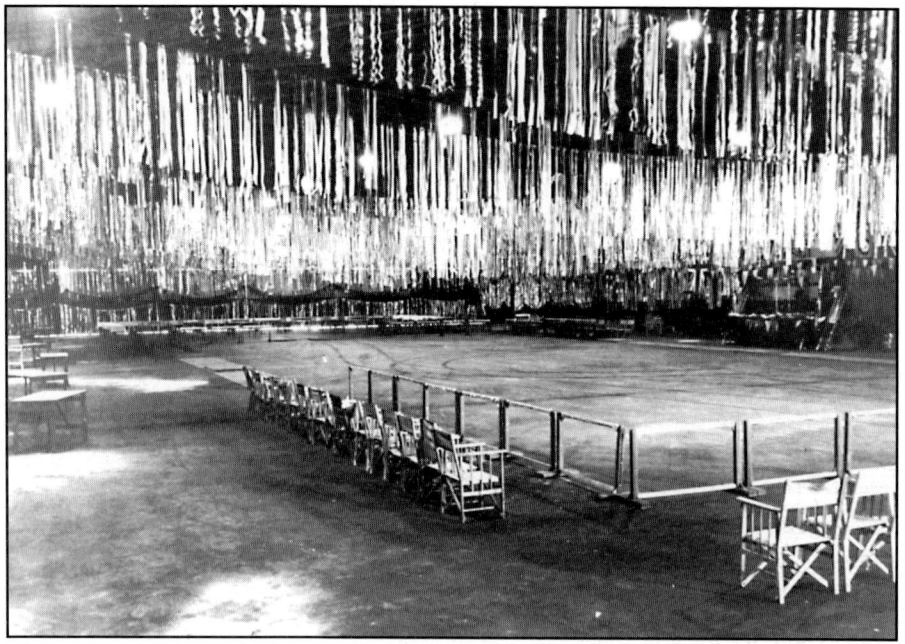

The Repair and Inspection hangar decorated with 'window' ready for the VE Day celebrations

Chapter 10
PREPARATIONS FOR TIGER FORCE

With the War in Europe at an end preparations were in hand to deal with the expected surplus personnel, not all would be needed for duty in the Far East. Names had been drawn up on the Release Scheme depending on individual's circumstances, those from the Commonwealth being amongst the earliest to be released. Within two weeks after VE day the WAAFs were given a talk on the WAAF Release and Resettlement Scheme designed to help them readjust to life in civvy street and to find suitable work. Courses in the Education Block were available to all personnel who wanted to take advantage of the Educational and Vocational Training Scheme offering subjects such as english, mathematics and shorthand. Earlier in the year a discussion about 'The woman's place after the war' had received unanimous agreement amongst the WAAFs that their place was at home. However one WAAF who was amongst the first release found, after only two weeks, that civvy street was not so comfortable and she wished she were back with her friends at Metheringham. The first airman, of release group 1, left Metheringham on June 20, although another group had already left two weeks earlier, when 1690 BDTF departed for RAF Syerston, its job at Metheringham completed.

Relaxation in some areas of discipline allowed, for example, the WAAFs to wear sports clothes when cycling and going swimming and made a welcome change, the chance to 'show a leg' was enjoyed equally by the RAF and by the WAAFs! No longer being constrained by operations meant that more time was available for entertainment and the St. Georges Players gave another performance of the Lesley Storm comedy play Tony Draws a Horse which had been well received at its premier performance early in May. The newly formed Entertainments Committee tried to bring a little more variety to the social scene and were particularly pleased with the enthusiastic reception given to an ENSA musical concert, an evening mainly of opera,

Members of the St Georges Players in a scene from 'Tony Draws a Horse'

followed a week later by a performance by the Ballet Guild. F/O Ibbitt, whose gramophone club had been such a popular Sunday evening feature for the past eighteen months, was posted, F/Sgt Brown and LAC Payne taking over the reigns, whilst the recently introduce 'Other Ranks' dances in the NAAFI regularly attracted between one hundred and twenty and one hundred and fifty keen dancers.

Attention now turned to the war with Japan. Winston Churchill had pledged Britain's resources towards the defeat of Japan once Germany had been overwhelmed and plans had already been drawn up to deploy aircraft to the Far East as an additional British and Commonwealth contribution under the code name 'Tiger Force'.

On the 16th June nineteen aircraft of 467 Squadron flew the ten miles from Waddington to take up residence at Metheringham joining 106 to form 552 Wing. The Australians were greeted on arrival with barrels of beer, courtesy of 106 Squadron but, needless to say, they were rather unimpressed with Metheringham having become accustomed to the comforts of the pre-war station at Waddington. The Squadron's ground staff also transferred creating some difficulty in finding accommodation for everyone, since Metheringham had been built as a single squadron Station. Indeed those who drew the short straw found themselves living, and working, in tents, fortunately it was summer. *'The English climate never becomes monotonous, it changes every hour, heatwave, rain and fog at night - all in one day!'* and *'...the three quarters of a mile walk from the messes to the flight offices should be quite stimulating if the English summer behaves'* summed up the Aussies thoughts of their new home.

John Dawson, posted to 467 in July 1945 from 6 Group '..*found flight work rather dull. There was no longer the hustle and bustle of activity associated with wartime operations. I found myself filling in time learning to kick an Australian rugby type football alongside the Australian ground crew on the flight. I do recall being shown with some pride a Lancaster with over 100 operations to its credit. This was of course PO : S-Sugar now a prize exhibit in the Bomber Command Hall at the RAF Museum Hendon.'* R5868 had served with 83 Squadron before joining 467 Squadron in September 1943 and completing one hundred and thirty seven sorties by the end of the war in Europe.

An athletics meeting between the two Squadrons organised for 11th July took place in typical English summer weather *'Raining - extremely bad light with ground mist, reminiscent of Melbourne at its best. Outlook for athletic meeting very poor, but weather improved slightly by midday and, in spite of heavy going, it was decided to hold the meeting'.* 467 Squadron's ORB went on to record *'Despite the elements and No. 106 Squadron aircrew, No. 467 Squadron aircrew had a very successful day and ultimately won the Athletic Shield in a very close finish. Special mention is made of two events which were outstanding, the tug of war and the three mile championship. In the former event No. 467 Squadron aircrew, by brute strength and propaganda, had no difficulty in reaching the final, which they eventually won on the third pull. After winning the toss for positions the team, prior to the third pull, returned to their original well prepared foxholes where they again dug in and resisted all No. 106 Squadron's strenuous efforts to dislodge them. In the three mile it was found that the Squadron did not have a representative and, shortly before the race, F/Sgt McKenzie was prevailed upon to enter in the hope of gaining a few extra points. McKenzie ran an excellently judged race and took the lead in the last lap, and despite a strong challenge by the representative of No. 106 Squadron aircrew, put in a magnificent finish to run out an easy winner'.* Mrs. McMullen, the Station Commander's wife, presented trophies to individual winners and the Athletic Shield to 467 Squadron.

The Fighter Command airfield at RAF Digby used Blankney Hall as a Sector Operations Room. Located less than two miles from RAF Metheringham it provided some light relief for crews on training flights when it was discovered that the WAAFs based there were enjoying nude sunbathing on the roof of the old Hall. Although unseen from the ground they were quite visible to crews of low flying aircraft, word soon spread and low flying in the vicinity increased until, following complaints from villagers, the rooftop sunbathing was stopped. One Sunday afternoon in mid

July fire broke out in an upstairs linen cupboard and quickly spread through the old Hall. John Woodrow, taking a water tanker from Metheringham, joined many others in fighting the fire but without success, the old Hall was irreparably damaged, although within a few days the Operations Room was back in action in a wing, a later addition to the Hall, which had been virtually untouched.

By now both Squadrons had exchanged aircraft, with units within 8 Group, receiving newer aircraft fitted with the latest radar developments. 'Bullseyes', training flights, became a regular feature bringing crews back to peak operational efficiency and developing familiarity with their new equipment. Sgt John Rogers recalls one on 23rd July when *'The exercise took us out over the North Sea, south across the coast of Belgium, over France and back across the Channel, thence to a bombing range off the Welsh coast in Cardigan Bay where we dropped a practice bomb and thence back to base. From what I recall all the radar on the 'plane went out of order and we didn't seem to be able to get decent radio bearings, so I had to rely on a couple of map readings when we crossed the coast. Even so we bombed on time and arrived back at base on time. More good luck than good judgement.'* Jean Danford collected one crew from their aircraft after a training flight *'When they got out of the plane at the dispersal they were very shaken and one young man smelled awful. When I asked what the smell was they laughed. The crew had had a very close shave as over the sea all four engines had suddenly cut out, the aircraft dived towards the sea losing a great deal of height before they were restarted. They said that during the incident the elsan, which was fixed at the back of the 'plane, had tipped its contents all over him. The poor chap looked most embarrassed.'*

During a series of 'quick landing' exercises 106 Squadron put up a best time of three minutes and two seconds to land six aircraft whilst 467 Squadron could only manage a best time of three minutes and eighteen seconds. This high level of training was not without its hazards and within a space of four days two of 106's Lancasters suffered accidents, one bursting a tyre on landing and damaging the FIDO pipes, the rear gunner being slightly injured and another belly landing across the runway whilst practising three engined overshooting, again damaging the FIDO pipes, a small fire was quickly extinguished.

Rumours persisted that the Wing was to be sent overseas very soon, the destination Okinawa, and this seemed to be born out when medical examinations and inoculations were administered prior to embarkation leave for those officers and men selected. However the dropping of the nuclear bombs on Hiroshima and Nagasaki, on 6th and 9th August, by B29s of the USAAF signalled the Japanese surrender. John Rogers recalls that on the night of

In the Middle of Nowhere - *The History of RAF Metheringham*

14th August *'..we were about to retire for the night when we heard over the tannoy that the war was over. Most of us headed for the Sergeants' Mess in an excited frame of mind. A few officers and NCOs took Verey pistols from the aircraft and fired signal flares into the air to try and land them on the other Mess. These were fairly close together and as they were Romney huts made of curved corrugated iron there was not much danger. The Station Commander obviously sensed danger and I recall him arriving in the Sergeants' Mess to confiscate the pistols. He must have been wary of trouble as he brought the Padre along for moral support. Some of the Australians had broken open the bar and literally rolled out the barrel. The President of the Messing Committee, who lived in the Mess grabbed the cash box and locked himself in his room. The CO did not try to stop the celebration and accepted a pint of beer'.* John Dawson adds that the announcement *'.....sparked off a wave of activity. The grass around the site huts had been cut and was quite dry and piles of it were heaped up and set fire to in celebration. It was said that the Australians set fire to a hay stack and followed this up by setting fire to the fire engine sent to put it out.'* Pre-empting any further trouble all flying was restricted, vehicles and aircraft were immobilised and all Verey pistols and cartridges securely locked up!

VJ Day itself followed a similar format to VE Day and the local villagers were again invited to join the Station personnel for a celebration dance in the Repair and Inspection hangar. John Dawson found that there wasn't a great deal going on and that many were taking the opportunity to leave the Station. Melton Mowbray, his home town, was not too far away and he and a friend decided to surprise his family, *'With some difficulty we hitched most of the way and arrived in time for tea to the delight of my parents. That evening the pair of us joined the local celebrations in the market place where we met up with some of my friends. Eventually we were invited home with them and entertained until about 2 o'clock in the morning'*

Chapter 11
THE FINAL MONTHS

On his return to Metheringham the following day John Dawson found that there was still little activity *'How long this inactivity lasted I can't recall but when eventually some sort of semblance of order returned it was decided that the ground staff of 467 Squadron should be rewarded by being flown to the Victory Test Match* (England v Australia) *then being held at Old Trafford. Each day of the test match the Squadron's aircraft took those whose names were drawn out of a hat for that day. George* (George Tucker, posted to Metheringham with John, and who had recently taken over the music club held in the YMCA) *and myself were allotted places in PO-W of B Flight along with about eighteen others. Though Ringway was nearest to the cricket ground we were due to land at Burton Wood. The trip was uneventful until, as we neared the Pennines, someone near me in an excited state pointed out of the window along the wing at the starboard inner engine. This was pouring out smoke and flames. We were ordered to put our parachutes on. After what seemed an age we made a three engined landing on Ringway's main runway. We bounced about three times before coming to rest having run off the end of the runway with our wheels in some barbed wire defences and our nose over a concrete pillbox. We poured out of the aircraft in a state of great excitement. Of the match I remember nothing but I do remember having to make our way to Burton Wood and flying back to Metheringham in another aircraft and without a parachute!'*

Although the flying restriction imposed on VJ Day was lifted two days later very little flying took place for the remainder of the month. Jean Danford on duty one night at the end of the month was driving her crew bus to dispersals to await Lancasters returning from a training flight *' I had seen a Lancaster coming in my direction when suddenly nothing it had vanished! I was not fond of the dark in those days and had heard stories of ghost planes and naturally I thought I had witnessed one. I dashed back to the MT yard to be*

In the Middle of Nowhere - *The History of RAF Metheringham*

told I hadn't seen a ghost plane but in fact one had gone over the end of the runway.' The 467 Squadron Lancaster had landed well along the main runway and disappeared off the northern end, where the ground fell away down to the level of the surrounding fields, and came to rest one hundred and fifty yards into this area of rough ground undamaged and without injury to the crew. Having finally been convinced that the 'plane she had seen was real, Jean returned to collect the crew who had by then reached the perimeter track on foot having left their aircraft where it had come to rest. Jean also recalls that the WAAFs were given the opportunity to have a flight in a Lancaster *'We had to get permission to do so then we were taught how to use a parachute and the way to fall from a plane - thank goodness it was on the ground at the time! I don't know whether it was to try to put us off, however, I went up with F/Lt 'Bing' Emerson's crew, we went to Cardigan Bay to jettison some bombs. It was a beautiful day and a really wonderful experience I will never forget, the blue sky, white clouds edged with gold from the sun and the various yellows and greens of the fields below. I cherish that memory because it was the first time I had flown and to top it in a beautiful and famous bomber.'*

As well as disposing of surplus bombs at sea they were also delivered, by road, to designated storage depots. John Woodrow, taking a load to a depot in Derbyshire, was driving his lorry through Ashbourne when, rounding a corner, a 500lb bomb fell of the trailer he was towing and rolled to a stop at the feet of several people standing in a queue at a 'bus stop. Having stopped his lorry he stood scratching his head wondering how he was going to load the offending bomb back onto the trailer when, by a stroke of good fortune, an RAF mobile crane appeared from around the corner.

The war now over there was no longer a need for 552 Wing and it was officially disbanded on 28th August.

Throughout September 106 were involved in 'Operation Dodge' to repatriate POWs from Italy. Aircraft flew to Bari in southern Italy to collect troops and during their time on the ground crews took the opportunity to enjoy the warm weather swimming and local sight seeing. The six and a half hour flight back to the reception centre at Tibenham was uncomfortable with twenty passengers crammed in like sardines and had to be made at below 10,000 ft as there was no additional oxygen supplies for the passengers. One ex-POW grinned with delight having been given the opportunity to sit in the mid upper turret declaring the view to be *'just like fairyland'* it being his first flight.

Fred Girkin recalls that they also flew servicewomen home from Bari and in such cases the normally open Elsan toilet was screened by a hessian curtain to preserve their modesty. On a particularly bumpy flight home his

Lancaster suddenly 'dropped' causing the hessian screen to rise, much to the embarrassment of the ATS girl comfortably seated on the Elsan and to the amusement of the male passengers.

John Rogers took part in Operation Spasm, to Berlin *'I am unsure of the object of this exercise, we were told it was to let us see the damage done to Berlin by the RAF, which seems unlikely. We also flew a few service people from Tibenham to Berlin and others on the return journey. Our route took us over Lowestoft across the North Sea and Holland, over Hanover and Magdeburg, to Gatow airfield in the British sector of Berlin. At that time Gatow was grass with no concrete runways. Take off and landing was a very bumpy affair. While we were in Berlin we were able to walk around quite freely into the different sectors. We did not make any serious attempt to talk to the Russian soldiers but I had a feeling they were a bit wary of making contact. I can't remember much about the city except the scenes of devastation. Fraternisation with the Germans was forbidden, of course, but I was impressed that they seemed to be coping as well as people in this country did during and after the Blitz.'*

On 30th September 467 Squadron disbanded at Metheringham and the Australians returned home. Shortly before they departed the 106 Squadron crest was taken from its place of honour in the Officers' Mess and, although 467 were suspected of the disappearance, a thorough search failed to reveal its whereabouts.

Mid October saw more arrivals at Metheringham. 189 Squadron had been formed at Bardney in October 1944, moving to Fulbeck the following month it had returned to Bardney in early April 1945. Arriving over Metheringham during mid-afternoon on 15th October seventeen Lancasters attempted to land but had some difficulties due to poor visibility. Permission was given to light FIDO and, once the smoke cleared, all were able to land safely. Their stay was very short as on 20th November the Squadron disbanded once again leaving 106 as the only resident unit.

Three days later a special all ranks dance in the NAAFI honoured the return of Sgt (now Warrant Officer) Norman Jackson, VC together with three members of his crew who had been shot down in April 1944. Having spent ten months in hospital he had been transferred to a prisoner of war camp, from where he successfully escaped on his second attempt. He then managed to get through the German lines and make contact with American troops near Munich. Around six hundred people saw the Squadron Commander, W/Cdr Levis, present a tankard to Jackson and other mementos to F/O Higgins (navigator), W/O Sandilands (wireless operator) and W/O Toft (bomb aimer). Jean Danford asked W/O Jackson for his autograph and he duly obliged adding the simple quotation "God is my guide" which

Jean remembers *'said so much in those days'*.

From 1st December Metheringham ceased to be a sub station of 54 Base, within 5 Group and came under the control of 1 Group which covered north Lincolnshire from its HQ at Bawtry. Coningsby transferred to 3 Group, with its HQ at Mildenhall.

The FIDO facility was withdrawn on 5th and the system decommissioned, all petrol held in the storage tanks on the airfield was pumped back to the railway siding at Metheringham railway station from where tankers took it to Carnaby and Woodbridge.

With the gradual decrease in personnel, who were being posted and 'demobbed' at the rate of around 300 a month, entertainments other than the cinema were becoming less frequent, ENSA shows were now at two to three week intervals and dances also became less regular. A new venture however were 'whist drives' which raised money for Lord Southwood's appeal on behalf of the Great Ormond Street Childrens' Hospital. The Station Dance Band came very close to extinction on several occasions as the Station strength diminished but managed to survive thanks to some opportune recruitment. Winter again settled in and at a mid December dance in the Sergeants Mess it was noted that *'the low temperature communicated itself to the beer... not only the bitter cold but also cold bitter explains the surprisingly low consumption. Dancing was the only way of keeping warm.'*

The last Christmas at Metheringham was fairly low key as many of those remaining managed to get home on leave. A children's party in the YMCA

Sergeant Norman Cyril Jackson whose citation for the award of the Victoria Cross appeared in The London Gazette on 26th October 1945 (he then held the rank of Warrant Officer)

on Christmas Eve was followed by a carol service. An all ranks dance in the NAAFI welcomed in the New Year.

By now the Air Traffic Control Centre at Uxbridge had been informed that the airfield would close at night and only be available during daylight hours for emergency landings. It is not certain but is possible that a Mosquito of Coastal Command from Mount Farm in Oxfordshire may have been in difficulty and trying to reach Metheringham when it crashed about four miles to the south, near Billinghay. The crash crew attended the scene where both occupants were found to have been killed.

The very last ENSA show, staged on 26th January, 'Alfredo's Band' was considered *'...to be a grande finale to a whole range of shows some of which it must be admitted were mediocre but all of which had nevertheless done a great deal to lift the morale and relieve the tedium during the previous two years.'*

Flying training continued right up until official confirmation that 106 Squadron was to cease flying at 00.01 on 15th February and be disbanded with effect from 18th February 1946. A full Station parade on the main runway, at which W/Cdr Levis read out the notice of disbandment, marked the official end of the Squadron's existence. The unofficial end was a more memorable event in the form of a 'mock' funeral. A small 'coffin' containing a Squadron nominal roll and history and topped with an RAF cap was carried on a farmers dray, with only three wheels, to its last resting place close to the Squadron offices, accompanied by aircrew pallbearers. There it was lowered into the 'grave' after which W/Cdr Levis laid a laurel wreath, decorated with two one- pint beer tankards and a large brassiere stretched across the middle. This was accompanied by a traditional volley from the firing party over the grave and an aircrew trumpeter playing 'She'll be coming round the mountain when she comes' at the graveside. A white wooden cross bearing the inscription '106 Squadron 1917-1946' marked the grave and was later replaced by a grave stone inscribed '106 Squadron Royal Air Force 1917-1919 1938-1946 Pro Libertate'

By the end of the month all of the Squadron's Lancasters had gone, some to other units the remainder to be scrapped. S/L Bray, the Station Admin. Officer, assumed command on 22nd February when W/Cdr McDondal, who had replaced G/Cpt McMullen, transferred to Group HQ. Perhaps surprisingly the Station strength still stood at 770.

An unfortunate episode in late February occurred when an airman was admitted to Station Sick Quarters with a sore throat and found to be suffering from diptheria, he was immediately transferred to the isolation block at Cranwell where he died on 22nd February. Measures taken to prevent the spread of the infection were successful with no further cases occurring.

In the Middle of Nowhere - *The History of RAF Metheringham*

Scenes from the 106
Squadron Funeral...

...the procession...

...firing party and 'mourners' assembled...

...the grave

110

A simple cross and an impressive wreath marked the last resting place of 106 Squadron in a lighthearted ceremony

106 Squadron in February 1946

Ted Bullen, now responsible for running the Release Section, had the benefit of some high ranking assistants '..to *help me there was a number of aircrew personnel, from the rank of Squadron Leader down. As you can imagine, being in charge of the Release Section, I was very popular and in particular with the cookhouse. Myself and one or two of my colleagues could always get something to eat at any time.*' Releases continued and by mid March the majority of the WAAF contingent had been posted or released, the last airwoman, Sgt Walker, leaving on 31st March.

On April 16th a Board of Survey of the Station Headquarters files and historical documents commenced under the control of F/O S Dwight who assumed responsibility for the Station as it returned to Care and Maintenance status. A great deal of equipment had to be collected together ready for sending on to other stations or returned to be disposed of through surplus sales. The ubiquitous bicycles were hung up in the Repair and Maintenance hangar ready for collection while furniture, tables and bed linen were stacked in large piles and burnt. John Greensmith once again found himself on 'jankers' after passing some derisory comment, whilst stacking chairs, and spent a fortnight doing the washing up.

By the end of July the C&M party had also departed and so after just over two and a half years of intense activity on this temporary wartime airfield a stillness returned to this corner of Lincolnshire.

Saying Goodbye

We've been friends and worked together through
the war's grim days - Now the job is finished and
we go our separate ways...... Thanks for being such
a pal; the best I ever knew. This is where we say
goodbye. But I'll remember you.

There were times when things were bad and dark
clouds hid the sun. But we made the best of it and
we had lots of fun..... It's over now, and maybe we
shall never meet again - But always in my memory
our friendship will remain.

Patience Strong

FIDO

NUMBER TWO.   MARCH, 1946

FACT, FICTION, FUN,
INTERESTING
DIGEST
OF

PRICE SIX PENCE

METHERINGHAM MAGAZINE

The Station magazine FIDO, started belatedly in 1946, ran to only two issues

Chapter 12
EPILOGUE

Local people soon found that they were able to walk around the various dispersed sites quite freely and, unsurprisingly, useful items were 'liberated'. Baskets full of pots, pans and crockery soon found new owners and rolls of linoleum provided a welcome new floor covering in many homes. The impression gained by many local people is that the Station just seemed to be abandoned and they were surprised at what had been left behind, syringes and other medical items in the sick quarters, boxes of flares in the control tower and bombs in the bomb store. Rosie Harrad found books and paper which she and other children used for drawing and writing on and in the bomb aiming training building, as well as the equipment, there were hundreds of photographs and negatives, which the children threw into the air to create their own snowstorm.

The empty Nissen huts and temporary brick buildings quickly attracted squatters since housing accommodation was in very short supply and within a short space of time people were living all over the airfield. John Woodrow and his wife Mary moved into the guardroom and when John started his new job in 'civvy street' as an AA patrolman he kept his motorcycle and sidecar in the fire tender shed on the opposite side of the road. John also had a motorcycle as personal transport and soon found that the FIDO pipeline still contained petrol and although of fairly low quality his motorcycle could be persuaded to run reasonably well on it. On one occasion he was sawing down a telegraph pole near the sick quarters picket post when he was surprised by the local policeman who had been hiding inside. Thinking quickly he explained that the wire made an excellent aerial for his radio, the policeman thought that this was a good idea and helped himself to some as well. John returned later to collect the pole for firewood.

In February 1947 the Communal and Mess sites were transferred to the Ministry of Agriculture and Fisheries and in November of the same year it

In the Middle of Nowhere - *The History of RAF Metheringham*

Workers at the Voluntary Agricultural Camp. Rosie Harrad, third left centre row and Mr Podesta the camp warden, extreme left centre row

115

In the Middle of Nowhere - *The History of RAF Metheringham*

The VAC dining room in the former NAAFI

VAC workers board their transport. The squash court and gymnasium are to the right of the lorry, whilst the standby generator house can be seen in the background

was recommended that the Station be abandoned and returned to agriculture, although it proved to be a further nine years before any action was taken.

The Ministry of Agriculture used the communal site as a Voluntary Agricultural Camp where ordinary people were able to spend a week or two on a working holiday providing a source of labour for the local farms. They were taken by lorry each morning to the days work and collected each evening. Once the days work had been done their time was their own and many social activities took place, including bus trips to Skegness on a Sunday and dances in the old NAAFI where the wooden dance floor still survived and where the former restaurant served as the VAC dining room. At this time Rosie Harrad, a member of staff at the VAC remembers that many of the visitors returned regularly each year and that a number were from countries occupied by the Germans during the war. The VAC continued until around 1955/56.

In January 1956 it was finally confirmed that there was no longer a requirement for the airfield and the release of 321 acres held on requisition was authorised. This represented about half of the airfield site the remainder being state owned. Later that year the two T2 hangars were earmarked for transfer to the Hebrides, for what purpose is not clear, but were then declared surplus to requirements. Meanwhile an offer of £4000 pounds for the B1 hangar, by a Leeds firm, had been declined. All three were eventually sold and removed from site in 1958 although prior to this they had been put to use for corn storage.

East Kesteven Rural District Council had made arrangements with the Air Ministry to take over three of the quarters site, on the road into Martin, to provide temporary housing. Each Nissen hut was converted into two units, each unit having two bedrooms, a living room, bathroom and kitchen, cooking was by a solid fuel stove. A communal wash house meant that laundry arrangements were on a rota basis. At the time the accommodation was considered reasonably comfortable and the council had installed wooden windows and lined the huts with plasterboard, the exterior being covered with hessian and tarred. With a weekly rent of 7/6d these temporary homes were very soon filled, the site being known locally as 'Tin Town'. In the mid fifties the Council then built permanent housing on one of the sites, West Grove, and together with other new housing in the area meant that the old quarters were no longer required and all were vacated by the end of 1958.

RAF Coningsby had undertaken a 'parenting' responsibility for Metheringham since its closure and maintained this supervisory role until

Mrs Baumber and Mrs Creasey outside the converted quarters at Moor Grove

October 1958. The local Electricity Board commenced transferring its customers, who were still fed through the Air Ministry system, to its own network whilst the GPO had recovered its poles and cables and abandoned the ducts by November 1959.

With no further need for 'Tin Town' the scrap merchants moved in and by the early sixties all of the temporary housing units, including the FIDO tanks, had been removed.

The main airfield site continued to see 'service' activity of a slightly different kind being regularly used by the Territorial Army for manoeuvres and weekend camps and by the Civil Defence for exercises.

In 1960 roads were reopened across the airfield to replace the two lost when construction started in 1943. After consultation with the local parish councils it was agreed that to reinstate the original roads would be too costly, so a strip of the East-West runway was converted into a public road for most of its length together with that part of the perimeter track southward towards the Martin road.

To the west of the airfield the Communal, Admin. and Sick Quarters buildings were taken over by local farmers for produce and implement storage while small businesses grew up on the Technical Site.

Flying continued on and off for some time as visiting pleasure flight operators sought to encourage people from surrounding villages to take to the air. More regular use was made of the runways at Metheringham, and many other abandoned airfields, by crop sprayers, until the main and NW-SE runways were broken up for hardcore in the early 1970s.

Roy Bradley who was the only survivor of JB601, shot down in April 1944, had been badly injured but was looked after by the Resistance at Laneuville a Bayard until he was captured. Since the War he had revisited the airfield several times and, having maintained contact with former members of the Resistance had shown their wartime leader around the Station from which he had flown on his first and only 'op'. They had presented him with several parts recovered from V-Victor's crash site including a fuel pump from one of the Merlin engines. In turn Roy Bradley presented the pump to the original owners of V-Victor, Cyril Ginder's crew who had flown twenty one of their last twenty two 'ops' on this Lancaster and which had carried their nose art. In 1972 Roy Bradley learned of the existence of the gravestone still in place at the site of the mock funeral. With the agreement of the landowner, Peter South, he arranged for the gravestone to be removed to Newark Air Museum for safekeeping.

In the mid 1970s the now retired Air Commodore Levis, who as a Wing Commander had been 106 Squadron's CO at the time of its disbandment,

Harry Stunell (middle) and Ron Needle (right) at the dedication ceremony at Meligny le Grand in May 1990. Tom Renoue (left) was a friend of the crew's pilot James Scott

had been invited to a cocktail party at RAF Waddington where he met a number of Australians who were in England visiting their wartime airfields. He discovered from a group of ex-467 Squadron aircrew, who had been stationed at Metheringham in 1945, that the 106 Squadron crest had indeed been liberated by members of 467 Squadron and had spent the last thirty years in Australia. It was duly presented, undamaged and carefully preserved, to A/Cdr Levis who returned it to the care of the RAF.

In 1983 a small grass strip in the north eastern corner of the airfield was used for flying micro light aircraft. This operation gradually expanded and boasted several machines and a small hangar before closing in the mid 1990s.

During the 1980s the line of a new gas supply pipeline passed through part of the airfield site. The contractors, being aware of the story of the steam roller and the caterpillar tractor, searched for but did not find them

In 1986 Ron Needle visited Meligny le Grand for the first time since 1945, there he found that the memories of the crash were still very much in the minds of the local people. He also met Andre Fromont who had been ringing the church bell, the sound of the Angelus, which led to both his and Harry Stunnel's survival in the bitter cold of that January morning. Friendships quickly developed in the village and Ron returned in 1989 accompanied by Harry and they have continued to make regular visits. In May 1990 a plaque, dedicated to the memory of the crew was unveiled at a ceremony in the village church.

One evening early in 1990 Bill Winter received a telephone call, upon answering he was surprised and delighted to hear the voice of Harry Stunnel to whom he had last spoken forty five years before in the locker rooms at Metheringham. Following that telephone call they were able to renew their friendship and maintain regular contact.

In 1991 a memorial to 106 Squadron was unveiled on the eastern perimeter track close to the cottages in which Rosie Harrad and Walt Sewell had lived. The memorial, built by John Pye, incorporated the gravestone which had been returned from Newark Air Museum. A planned fly-past by the Battle of Britain Memorial Flight Lancaster was cancelled at the last minute due to technical difficulties, but one of Metheringham's own aircraft was scrambled and the microlight provided a memorable substitute scattering poppies as it made a low fly-past.

Peter Scoley returned to Martin Moor in 1968, not to Holme Farm but to Westmoor Farm on which the Communal site had been built. He and his wife had long dreamt of developing some lasting memorial to RAF Metheringham and the opportunity came in 1993 when North Kesteven District Council, the successor to East Kesteven Rural District Council, sponsored the restoration and development of an original temporary brick building into a Visitor Centre recounting the history of the airfield and remembering those men and women who were stationed there.

The 106 Squadron memorial on the former eastern perimeter track. The cottages where Mrs Harrad and Walt Sewell lived still stand

APPENDIX A
STATION COMMANDERS

S/Ldr Gordon, DFC 20.10.43-06.11.43
(CO and Admin. Officer during Care and Maintenance)

S/Ldr J Whattam 07.11.43-10.11.43
(CO and Admin. Officer during Care and Maintenance)

G/Cpt W N McKechnie, GC 11.11.43-29.08.44

W/Cdr E K Piercy 30.08.44-04.09.44
(Temporary Command)

G/Cpt M L Heath 05.09.44-27.06.45

G/Cpt C C McMullen, AFC 28.06.45-02.12.45

W/Cdr L G Levis .... 03.12.45-?
(Temporary Command)

W/Cdr McDondal .... ?-   21.02.46

S/Ldr Bray 22.02.46-17.04.46
(Station Admin. Officer)

F/O Dwight .... 18.04.46-?.07.46

106 SQUADRON COMMANDERS (AT METHERINGHAM)

W/Cdr R E Baxter, DFC .... March 1944

W/Cdr E K Piercy .... March 1944-August 1944

W/Cdr M M J Stevens, DFC August1944-March 1945

W/Cdr L G Levis .... March 1945-February 1946

APENDIX B
SUMMARY OF 106 SQUADRON OPERATIONS FROM RAF METHERINGHAM

1943

DATE	LOCATION	TARGET	DETAILED	DESPATCHED	LOST
18/19 NOV	BERLIN	Residential/Industrial	13	13	0
22/23 NOV	BERLIN	Resiidential/Industrial	17	17	0
23/24 NOV	BERLIN	Resiidential/Industrial	5	5	0
26/27 NOV	BERLIN	Residential/Industrial	18	18	1
2/3 DEC	BERLIN	Residential/Industrial	16	16	1
3/4 DEC	LEIPZIG	Residentail/Industrial	13	13	0
16/17 DEC	BERLIN	Residential/Industrial	15	15	1
20/21 DEC	FRANKFURT	Residential/Indusrtial	17	17	0
23/24 DEC	BERLIN	Residential/Industrial	17	10	0
29/30 DEC	BERLIN	Residential/Industrial	16	16	0

1944

DATE	LOCATION	TARGET	DETAILED	DESPATCHED	LOST
1/2 JAN	BERLIN	Residential/Industrial	15	15	2
2/3 JAN	BERLIN	Residential/Industrial	12	8	0
5/6 JAN	STETTIN	Residential/Industrial	11	11	0
14/15 JAN	BRUNSWICK	Residential/Industrial	14	14	0
20/21 JAN	BERLIN	Residential/Industrial	16	16	0
21/22 JAN	MAGDEBURG	Residential/Industrial	16	8	0
	BERLIN	Diversionary raid	1	1	0
27/28 JAN	BERLIN	Residential/Industrial	17	17	0
28/29 JAN	BERLIN	Residential/Industrial	17	17	0
30/31 JAN	BERLIN	Residential/Industrial	17	17	1
15/16 FEB	BERLIN	Residential/Industrial	19	19	0
19/20 FEB	LEIPZIG	Residential/Industrial	15	15	1
20/21 FEB	STUTTGART	Residential/Industrial	13	13	0
24/25 FEB	SCWEINFURT	Ballbearing factories/ residential areas	17	17	0
25/26 FEB	AUGSBURG	Residential/Industrial	15	15	0
1/2 MAR	STUTTGART	Residential/Industrial	16	16	0
10/11 MAR	CHATEAUROUX	Aircraft Factory	10	10	0
15/16 MAR	STUTTGART	Residential/Industrial	11	11	0
	WOIPPY ABANDONED	Aero engine factory	6	6	0
16/17 MAR	CLERMONT FARRAND	Michelin tyre factory	6	6	0

In the Middle of Nowhere - *The History of RAF Metheringham*

Date	Target	Type			
18/19 MAR	FRANKFURT	Residential/Indusrtial	13	13	0
	BERGERAC	Explosives factory	6	6	0
20/21 MAR	ANGOULEME	Explosives factory	6	6	0
22/23 MAR	FRANKFURT	Residential/Industrial	18	18	1
23/24 MAR	LYONS	Aero engine factory ABANDONED	6	6	0
24/25 MAR	BERLIN	Residential/Industrial	14	14	0
25/26 MAR	LYONS	Aero engine factory	6	6	0
26/27 MAR	ESSEN	Residential/Industrial	17	17	0
29/30 MAR	LYONS	Aero engine factory	4	4	0
30/31 MAR	NUREMBURG	Residential/Industrial	17	17	3
5/6 APR	TOULOUSE	Aircraft factory	12	12	0
9/10 APR	BALTIC	'Gardening'	8	8	0
	KONIGSBERGER	'Gardening'	3	3	0
10/11 APR	TOURS	Railway yards	11	11	0
11/12 APR	AACHEN	Residential/Industrial	7	7	0
18/19 APR	JUVISY	Railway yards	9	8	0
	STETTIN BAY	'Gardening'	9	9	0
20/21 APR	LA CHAPELLE	Railway yards	18	18	0
22/23 APR	BRUNSWICK	Residential/Industrial	20	20	1
24/25 APR	MUNICH	Residential/Industrial	17	16	0
26/27 APR	SCHWEINFURT	Residential/Industrial	16	16	5
1/2 MAY	TOULOUSE	Explosives/aircraft factories	12	12	0
3/4 MAY	MAILLY LE CAMP	Military camp	12	12	0
7/8 MAY	SALBRIS	Ammunition dump	12	12	4
9/10 MAY	GENNEVILLIERS	Aero engine factory	12	12	2
11/12 MAY	BOURG-LEOPOLD	Military camp	8	8	0
19/20 MAY	TOURS	Railway yards	16	16	0
21/22 MAY	DUISBURG	Residential/Industrial	6	6	0
	KIEL BAY	'Gardening'	12	12	0
22/23 MAY	BRUNSWICK	Residential/Industrial	18	18	1
27/28 MAY	NANTES	Rail junction/workshops	10	10	0
		'Gardening'	5	5	0
31 MAY 1 JUN	MAISY, NORMANDY	Gun Battery RECALLED	12	12	0
2/3 JUN	PAS DE CALAIS	Gun battery	3	3	0
	PAS DE CALAIS	Gun battery RECALLED	12	12	0
4/5 JUN	MAISY	Gun batery	3	3	0
5/6 JUN	ST PIERRE DU MONT	Gun battery	16	16	0
6/7 JUN	CAEN	Road bridges	14	14	2
8/9 JUN	RENNES	Railway yards	12	12	0
10/11 JUN	ORLEANS	Railway yards	8	8	0
	ORLEANS	Railway line to north	10	10	0
12/13 JUN	POITIERS	Railway station	17	17	0
14/15 JUN	AUNAY SUR ODON	Troop positions	20	20	0
15/16 JUN	CHATELLERAULT	Fuel dump	20	20	0
18/19 JUN	WATTEN	V1 store RECALLED	16	16	0
21/22 JUN	WESSELING/ GELSENKIRCHEN	Synthetic oil plant	20	20	2
24/25 JUN	POMMEREVAL	V1 store	16	16	1

Date	Location	Target	Col1	Col2	Col3
27/28 JUN	VITRY	Railway yards	16	16	2
29 JUN	BEAUVOIR	V1 launch site	14	14	0
4/5 JUL	ST LEU D'ESSERENT	Underground V1 store	10	10	2
7/8 JUL	ST LEU D'ESSERENT	Underground V1 store	16	16	5
12/13 JUL	CULMONT	Railway junction	6	6	0
14/15 JUL	VILLENEUVE	Railway yards	10	10	0
15/16 JUL	NEVERS	Railway yards	9	9	0
18 JUL	CAEN	Troop positions	19	19	0
19 JUL	THIVERNEY	Supply dump	17	17	0
20/21 JUL	COURTRAI	Rail yards/junction	20	20	0
23/24 JUL	KIEL	Residential/port area	12	12	0
24/25 JUL	STUTTGART	Residential/Industrial	9	9	0
	DONGES	Oil storage depot	9	9	0
25 JUL	ST CYR	Airfield & signals depot	20	20	0
26/27 JUL	GIVORS	Railway yards	20	20	0
28/29 JUL	STUTTGART	Residential/Industrial	18	18	1
30 JUL	CAHAGNES	Troop positions RECALLED	20	20	0
31 JUL	RILLY LA MONTAGE	V1 store	11	11	0
	JOIGNY LA ROCHE	Railway yards	8	8	0
1 AUG	LE BRETEQUE	Vi site ABANDONED	5	5	0
	SIRACOURT	V1 site ABANDONED	12	12	0
2 AUG	TROSSY ST MAXIM	V1 store	19	19	0
3 AUG	TROSSY ST MAXIM	V1 store	16	16	0
5 AUG	ST LEU D'ESSERENT	Underground V1 store	18	18	0
6 AUG	LORIENT	Submarine pens	16	16	0
7 AUG	SECQUEVILLE LA CAMPAGNE		16	16	1
9/10 AUG	FORET DE CHATTELLERAULT	Oil storage installation	16	16	0
11 AUG	BORDEAUX	Submarine pens	6	6	0
11/12 AUG	GIVORS	Railway yards	12	12	0
12/13 AUG	BRUNSWICK	Residential/Industrial	8	8	0
	FALAISE	Troop positions	7	7	0
14 AUG	QUENSAY	Troop positions	10	10	0
	BREST	Cruiser 'GUEYPON'	8	8	0
15 AUG	GILSE RIJEN	Airfield	17	17	0
16/17 AUG	STETTIN	Port & industrial area	10	10	0
	STETTIN BAY	'Gardening'	6	6	0
18 AUG	L'ISLE ADAM	Supply depot	15	15	0
	BORDEAUX	Oil storage installation	4	4	0
25/26 AUG	DARMSTADT	Residential/Industrial	17	17	0
26/27 AUG	KONISBERG	Port area	14	14	0
	KONIGSBERG	'Gardening'	3	3	0
29/30 AUG	KONIGSBERG	Port area	18	18	2
31 AUG	AUCHY LES HESDIN	V2 store	16	16	0

In the Middle of Nowhere - *The History of RAF Metheringham*

Date	Target	Description			
3 SEP	DEELEN	Airfield	17	17	0
9/10 SEP	MONCHEN GLADBACH	Residential/Industrial	18	18	0
11 SEP	LE HAVRE	Troop positions	19	11	0
11/12 SEP	DARMSTADT	Residential/Industrial	20	20	1
12/13 SEP	STUTTGART	Residential/Industrial	13	13	0
17 SEP	BOULOGNE	Troop positions	16	16	0
18/19 SEP	BREMERHAVEN	Port & industrial area	16	16	0
19/20 SEP	RHEYDT	Residential/Industrial	18	18	2
23/24 SEP	DORTMUND-EMS CANAL	Aquaduct nr Ladbergen	16	16	1
26/27 SEP	KARLSRUHE	Residential/Industrial	13	13	0
27/28 SEP	KAISERLAUTERN	Residential/Industrial	13	13	0
4/5 OCT	BALTIC SEA	'Gardening'	5	5	0
5 OCT	WIHELMSHAVEN	Port & industrial areas	9	9	0
6/7 OCT	BREMEN	Shipyards/Res/Industrial	14	14	1
14/15 OCT	BRUNSWICK	Residential/Industrial	12	12	0
17 OCT	WEST KAPPELLE, WALCHEREN	Sea wall	8	8	0
19/20 OCT	NUREMBERG	Residential/Industrial	13	13	0
24/25 OCT	KATTEGAT	'Gardening'	10	10	0
28/29 OCT	BERGEN	Submarine pens	16	16	0
	BERGEN	'Gardening'	2	2	0
30 OCT	WALCHEREN	Gun batteries	6	6	0
1 NOV	HOMBERG	Synthetic oil plant	20	20	1
2/3 NOV	DUSSELDORF	Residential/Industrial	16	16	0
4/5 NOV	DORTMUND-EMS CANAL	Near Ladbergen	12	12	0
6/7 NOV	MITTELLAND CANAL	ABANDONED	18	18	1
11/12 NOV	HARBURG	Oil refinery/res/industrial	20	20	0
16 NOV	DUREN	Support to ground forces	19	19	0
21/22 NOV	DORTMUND-EMS CANAL	Near Ladbergen	21	21	0
22/23 NOV	TRONDHEIM ABANDONED	Submarine pens	14	14	0
	HELGOLAND	'Gardening'	6	6	0
26/27 NOV	MUNICH	Residential/Industrial	23	23	0
4/5 DEC	HEILBRONN	Residential/Industrial	22	22	1
6/7 DEC	GIESSEN	Railway yards/res/ind.	20	20	0
8 DEC	URFT DAM		14	14	0
9 DEC	URFT DAM	RECALLED	15	15	0
11 DEC	URFT DAM		15	15	0
13/14 DEC	HORTEN, OSLO	Cruiser 'EMDEN'	20	20	0
15/16 DEC	BALTIC SEA	'Gardening'	15	15	1
17/18 DEC	MUNICH	Railways/res/industrial	13	13	0
18/19 DEC	GYDNIA	Port & warships	14	14	1
21/22 DEC	KATTEGAT	'Gardening'	10	10	0
	SCHNEIDMUHL	Railway junction	2	2	0
28/29 DEC	OSLO FJORD	'Gardening'	12	11	0
30/31 DEC	HOUFFALIZE	Troop positions/armour	12	12	0

1945

DATE	LOCATION	TARGET	DETAILED	DESPATCHED	LOST
1 JAN	DORTMUND-EMS CANAL	Near Ladbergen	10	10	0
1/2 JAN	MITTLELAND CANAL	Near Gravenhorst	9	9	0
4/5 JAN	ROYAN	Troop positions	16	16	1
5/6 JAN	HOUFFALIZE	Road junction	12	12	0
6/7 JAN	GYDNIA	'Gardening'	5	5	0
7/8 JAN	MUNICH	Residntial/Industrial	16	16	1
13/14 JAN	POLITZ	Synthetic oil plant	10	10	0
	SWINEMUNDE	'Gardening'	4	4	0
14/15 JAN	LEUNA	Synthetic oil plant	12	12	1
16/17 JAN	BRUX	Synthetic oil plant	14	14	0
1/2 FEB	SIEGEN	Residential/Industrial	15	15	0
2/3 FEB	KARLSRUHE	Residential/Industrial	15	15	0
7/8 FEB	DORTMUND-EMS CANAL	Near Ladbergen	12	12	0
8/9 FEB	NEUBRANDEN-BURG	Residential/Industrial	9	9	0
	SWINEMUNDE	'Gardening'	6	6	0
13/14 FEB	DRESDEN	Support to ground forces	17	17	0
14/15 FEB	ROSITZ	Oil refinery	17	17	0
15/16 FEB	KATTEGAT	'Gardening'	4	4	0
19/20 FEB	BOHLEN	Synthetic oil plant	17	17	0
20/21 FEB	MITTLELAND CANAL	Near Grvenhorst ABANDONED	10	10	0
21/22 FEB	MITTLELAND CANAL	Near Gravenhorst	10	10	0
23/24 FEB	HORTEN, OSLO	Submarine pens/ships	12	12	0
24/25 FEB	OSLO FJORD	'Gardening'	10	10	0
3 MAR	OSLO FJORD	'Gardening'	6	6	0
5/6 MAR	BOHLEN	Synthetic oil plant	14	14	0
6/7 MAR	SASSNITZ	Shipping & port area	10	10	0
7/8 MAR	HARBURG	Oil refinery	13	13	0
11 MAR	ESSEN	Residential/Industrial	14	14	0
12 MAR	DORTMUND	Residential/Industrial	14	14	1
14/15 MAR	LUTZKENDORF	Synthetic oil plant	16	15	1
16/17 MAR	WURZBURG	Area	13	12	0
20/21 MAR	BOHLEN	Synthetic oil plant	16	16	0

In the Middle of Nowhere - *The History of RAF Metheringham*

21/22 MAR	HAMBURG	Oil refinery	15	15	0
23/24 MAR	WESEL	Support to ground forces	14	14	0
27 MAR	FARGE	Oil storage depot	14	14	0
4 APR	NORDHAUSEN	Barracks	18	18	0
7/8 APR	MOLBIS	Synthetic oil plant	9	9	0
8/9 APR	LUTZKENDORF	Synthetic oil plant	17	17	0
13/14 APR	KIEL BAY	'Gardening'	5	5	0
16/17 APR	PILSEN	Railway yards	14	11	0
23 APR	FLENSBERG	Port/railway yards ABANDONED	17	17	0
25/26 APR	TONSBERG	Oil refinery	16	16	0
	OSLO FJORD	'Gardening'	2	2	0

APPENDIX C
LOSSES FROM METHERINGHAM

Final column denotes the last resting place of those killed. Those whose resting place is unknown are commemorated on the RAF memorial at Runnymede.

26/27th November 1943 Berlin Lancaster JB592 ZN-W
F/O	J R C Hoboken	P	Killed	Durnbach
Sgt	G E Lucas	F/E	Killed	Durnbach
F/O	J P J Jenkins	Nav	Killed	Durnbach
P/O	J C Graham	AB	Killed	Durnbach
F/O	A W Read	W/Op	Killed	Durnbach
Sgt	E W Davies	MUG	Killed	Durnbach
F/O	H G Stuffin	RG	Killed	Durnbach

2nd/3rd December 1943 Berlin Lancaster ED874 ZN-?
P/O	R F Neil	P	Killed	Berlin
Sgt	M J Sheryn	F/E	Killed	Berlin
F/O	J F Harmes	Nav	Killed	Runnymede
F/O	G L Ashman	AB	Killed	Berlin
F/Sgt	T J Robertson	W/Op	Killed	Berlin
Sgt	R P Prothero	MUG	Killed	Berlin
Sgt	G H Stubbs	RG	Killed	Berlin

16/17th December 1943 Berlin Lancaster JB638 ZN-G
P/O	C H Storer	P	Killed	Reichswald
F/Sgt	J Coulton	F/E	Killed	Reichswald
F/Sgt	E G Grundy	Nav	Killed	Reichswald
F/Sgt	R E Hackett	AB	Killed	Reichswald
Sgt	F W Kite	W/Op	Killed	Reichswald
Sgt	C Frankish	MUG	Killed	Reichswald
Sgt	M J Martin	RG	Killed	Reichswald

30th December 1943 Berlin Lancaster ED593 ZN-Y
Sgt	A Braid	F/E	Killed	Cleish

Aircraft hit by flak near Bremen, F/O Leggett landed safely at Coltishall

In the Middle of Nowhere - *The History of RAF Metheringham*

1st/2nd January 1944 Berlin Lancaster JB645 ZN-F

P/O	E C Holbourn	P	Killed	Berlin
Sgt	H V Walmsley	F/E	Killed	Berlin
Sgt	E N Burton	Nav	Killed	Berlin
Sgt	T T Powell	AB	Killed	Berlin
Sgt	J H Dyer	W/Op	Killed	Berlin
Sgt	T H Mallett	MUG	Killed	Berlin
F/Sgt	S R Mattick	RG	Killed	Berlin

!st/2nd January 1944 Berlin Lancaster JB642 ZN-J

P/O	F H Garnett	P	Killed	Hanover
Sgt	D McLean	F/E	Killed	Hanover
F/Sgt	T J Thomas	Nav	Killed	Hanover
Sgt	E M Pease	AB	Killed	Hanover
Sgt	E Edge	W/Op	Killed	Hanover
Sgt	J A Withington	MUG	Killed	Hanover
Sgt	A E Elsworthy	RG	POW	

30th/31st January 1944 Berlin Lancaster ND336 ZN-Q

P/O	K H Kirkland	P	Killed	Vieland
Sgt	W G Mann	F/E	Killed	Vieland
Sgt	K W Barry	Nav	Killed	Vieland
F/O	J Inston	AB	Killed	Vieland
Sgt	D Naylor	W/Op	Killed	Vieland
Sgt	R J Winfindale	MUG	Killed	Vieland
Sgt	R J Charters	RG	Killed	Vieland

15/16th February 1944 Berlin Lancaster JB534 ZN-K

P/O	R W Dickerson	P	Killed	Thetford
Sgt	G H Boffey	F/E	Killed	Tipton
F/O	R H Lewis	Nav	Killed	Dagenham
F/Sgt	F O W Pauley	AB	Killed	Oakington
Sgt	W C Hills	W/Op	Killed	Greenwich
Sgt	B Krukowski	MUG	Survived	
F/O	W H C Ramsay	RG	Survived	

19/20th February 1944 Leipzig Lancaster ME630 ZN-P

F/O	E R F Leggett	P	Killed	Berlin
Sgt	E F Windeatt	F/E	POW	
F/O	N C F Bloy	Nav	POW	
F/O	F B Chubb	AB	POW	
Sgt	T H Jones	W/Op	POW	
P/O	S W Payne	MUG	POW	
Sgt	J C Harrison	RG	POW	

22nd/23rd March 1944 Frankfurt Lancaster JB648 ZN-B

P/O	E W Rosser	P	Killed	Durnbach
Sgt	E C Harris	F/E	Killed	Runnymede
F/Sgt	D White	Nav	Killed	Runnymede
Sgt	N J Goss	AB	Killed	Durnbach
Sgt	E C Sears	W/Op	Killed	Durnbach
Sgt	J E Charnock	MUG	POW	
Sgt	H D Steele	RG	Killed	Runnymede

30th/31st March 1944 Nuremburg Lancaster JB566 ZN-C

F/Sgt	T W J Hall	P	Killed	Hanover
Sgt	C M Beston	F/E	POW	
F/Sgt	R H G Parker	Nav	Killed	Hanover
F/Sgt	J T Gill	AB	Killed	Hanover
Sgt	R D Dack	W/Op	POW	
Sgt	G A Poole	MUG	Killed	Hanover
Sgt	G S Robertson	RG	Killed	Hanover

30th/31st March 1944 Nuremburg Lancaster ND585 ZN-J

P/O	W G Moxey	P	Killed	Hotton
Sgt	E H Woods	F/E	Killed	Hotton
F/Sgt	F Thompson	Nav	Killed	Hotton
Sgt	C A Matthews	AB	Killed	Hotton
Sgt	H W Richardson	W/Op	Killed	Hotton
P/O	J A Harris	MUG	Killed	Hotton
Sgt	J P MacKilligin	RG	Killed	Hotton

30th/31st March 1944 Nuremburg Lancaster ND535 ZN-Q

P/O	R Starkey	P	POW	
Sgt	J F Harris	F/E	Killed	Hanover
Sgt	C Roberts	Nav	Killed	Hanover
F/Sgt	W M Paris	AB	POW	
Sgt	G W Walker	W/Op	Killed	Hanover
Sgt	J Jamieson	MUG	Killed	Hanover
Sgt	M Ellick	RG	Killed	Hanover

22nd/23rd April 1944 Brunswick Lancaster JB567 ZN-E

F/Lt	J H S Lee	P	Killed	Reichswald
P/O	J L Tucker	2nd P	Killed	Reichswald
Sgt	S W Simes	FE	POW	
F/O	H K Langrish	Nav	Killed	Reichswald
P/O	H E Beven	AB	POW	
F/Sgt	H Grainger	W/Op	Killed	Reichswald
Sgt	T Monteith	MUG	Killed	Reichswald
F/Sgt	K V Terry	RG	Killed	Reichswald

In the Middle of Nowhere - *The History of RAF Metheringham*

26/27th April 1944 Schweinfurt Lancaster ND850 ZN-?
P/O	W G Fraser	P	POW	
Sgt	D Simpson	FE	POW	
WO	G Collins	Nav	POW	
P/O	H T Peebles	AB	Killed	Chauffort
Sgt	A MacKenzie	W/Op	POW	
P/O	J A Moffat	MUG	Killed	Chauffort
F/Sgt	J P Keenan	RG	Killed	Chauffort

26/27th April 1944 Schweinfurt Lancaster ME669 ZN-O
F/O	F M Mifflin	P	Killed	Durnbach
Sgt	N C Jackson	F/E	POW	
F/Sgt	L Higgins	Nav	POW	
F/Sgt	M Toft	AB	POW	
Sgt	E Sandelands	W/Op	POW	
Sgt	W Smith	MUG	POW	
F/Sgt	N H Johnson	RG	Killed	Durnbach

26/27th April 1944 Schweinfurt Lancaster ND853 ZN-J
P/O	C A Bishop	P	Killed	Durnbach
Sgt	H R Healey	FE	Killed	Durnbach
F/Sgt	D Burns	Nav	POW	
F/Sgt	A Pickstone	AB	Killed	Durnbach
Sgt	P J Daw	W/Op	Killed	Durnbach
P/O	H A Brad	MUG	Killed	Durnbach
P/O	W G Stevens	RG	Killed	Durnbach

26/27th April 1944 Schweinfurt Lancaster JB562 ZN-M
P/O	E C B Harper	P	Killed	Durnbach
Sgt	H Wild	FE	Killed	Durnbach
P/O	P Madore	Nav	Killed	Durnbach
F/O	J B Steggles	AB	POW	
Sgt	S R Reeve	W/Op	Killed	Durnbach
W/O2	G Bryson	MUG	Killed	Durnbach
Sgt	P Callaway	RG	POW	

26/27th April 1944 Schweinfurt Lancaster JB601 ZN-V
S/Ldr	A O Murdoch	P	Killed	Laneuville
Sgt	R Bradley	2nd P	POW	
Sgt	L G A Izod	FE	Killed	Laneuville
Sgt	H D Clark	Nav	Killed	Laneuville
F/Sgt	W F Evans	AB	Killed	Laneuville
P/O	W F Collins	W/Op	Killed	Laneuville
Sgt	E A Hatch	MUG	Killed	Laneuville
Sgt	J H Rees	RG	Killed	Laneuville

7/8th May 1944 Salbris Lancaster LL891 ZN-S
F/O	E R Penman	P	Killed	Orleans
F/O	L D Steylaerts	2nd P	Killed	Orleans
Sgt	R N Johnson	FE	Killed	Orleans
F/O	E L Sharp	Nav	Killed	Orleans
F/O	E O Aaron	AB	Killed	Orleans
F/Sgt	S R Patti	W/Op	Killed	Orleans
F/Sgt	R F Stubelt	MUG	Killed	Orleans
Sgt	J A Roberts	RG	Killed	Orleans

7/8th May 1944 Salbris Lancaster JB292 ZN-R
P/O	C A Bartlett	P	Killed	Orleans
Sgt	B D West	FE	Killed	Orleans
F/Sgt	R A Loretan	Nav	Killed	Orleans
F/Sgt	E C Fry	AB	Killed	Orleans
F/Sgt	H G Pratt	W/Op	Killed	Orleans
Sgt	R G Williams	MUG	Killed	Orleans
F/Sgt	G W Woodd	RG	Killed	Orleans

7/8th May 1944 Salbris Lancaster ND870 ZN-S
P/O	K R Warren	P	Killed	St.Doulchard
Sgt	R Shipley	FE	Killed	St.Doulchard
F/Sgt	W Currie	Nav	Killed	St.Doulchard
F/O	J Guile	AB	Killed	St.Doulchard
Sgt	M C Sewell	W/Op	Killed	St.Doulchard
Sgt	W R Kennedy	MUG	Killed	St.Doulchard
Sgt	E Long	RG	Killed	St.Doulchard

7/8th May 1944 Salbris Lancaster JB612 ZN-U
P/O	H K Rose	P	Killed	St. Viatre
Sgt	A A Taylor	FE	Killed	St. Viatre
F/O	L M Falkins	Nav	Killed	St. Viatre
Sgt	J F Smith	AB	POW	
Sgt	D G Allen	W/Op	Killed	St. Viatre
Sgt	P Friel	MUG	Killed	St. Viatre
Sgt	C Stephenson	RG	Killed	St. Viatre

9/10th May 1944 Gennevilliers Lancaster ND511 ZN-N
P/O	H A Sutherland	P	Killed	Clichy
Sgt	W Hall	FE	Killed	Clichy
F/Lt	R A C Hammond	Nav	Killed	Clichy
P/O	G McDougall	AB	Killed	Clichy
Sgt	A J McAllister	W/Op	Killed	Clichy
Sgt	R J Smith	MUG	Killed	Clichy
P/O	C H Shaw	RG	Killed	Clichy

9/10th May 1944 Gennevilliers Lancaster ND851 ZN-H

Rank	Name	Role	Fate	Location
P/O	J S Woodhams	P	Killed	Evreux
Sgt	W L Restell	FE	Killed	Evreux
F/Sgt	E Shepherd	Nav	Killed	Evreux
Sgt	E D James	AB	POW	
Sgt	E Anthony	W/Op	Killed	Evreux
Sgt	R F Toland	MUG	Killed	Evreux
P/O	R J Smith	RG	Killed	Evreux

22nd/23rd May 1944 Brunswick Lancaster ME790 ZN-U

Rank	Name	Role	Fate	Location
F/Lt	S J Houlden	P	Killed	Rheinberg
P/O	W H Scott	2nd P	Killed	Rheinberg
Sgt	R H Cozens	FE	Killed	Rheinberg
W/O	C H Whyte	Nav	Killed	Rheinberg
W/O	K T Millikan	AB	Killed	Rheinberg
W/O	G M Pringle	W/Op	POW	
Sgt	R C Hulme	MUG	Killed	Rheinberg
F/Sgt	S N Kelly	RG	Killed	Rheinberg

6/7th June 1944 Caen Lancaster NE150 ZN-M

Rank	Name	Role	Fate	Location
P/O	M G M Warren	P	Killed	Bayeux
Sgt	F L Corner	FE	Killed	Bayeux
F/O	J Drylie	Nav	POW	
F/Sgt	S R Black	AB	Killed	Bayeux
Sgt	N C V Rooker	W/Op	Killed	Bayeux
Sgt	M H Wigham	MUG	Killed	Bayeux
Sgt	R L Puckett	RG	Killed	Bayeux

6/7th June 1944 Caen Lancaster ND680 ZN-P

Rank	Name	Role	Fate	Location
S/Ldr	E Sprawson	P	POW	
Sgt	K Anderton	FE	POW	
F/O	R R C Barker	Nav	POW	
F/O	E L Hogg	AB	POW	
Sgt	W D Low	W/Op	POW	
F/O	P S Arnold	G	Killed	Runnymede
Sgt	E E J Wiggins	G	Killed	Runnymede

21st/22nd June 1944 Wesseling Lancaster LM570 ZN-Z

Rank	Name	Role	Fate	Location
F/O	K G Bellingham	P	Killed	Uden
S/Ldr	A J Loughborough	2nd P	Killed	Uden
Sgt	J W Blanchard	FE	Killed	Uden
F/Sgt	H Gavin	Nav	Killed	Uden
F/Sgt	L Toomey	AB	Killed	Uden
Sgt	A Goodacre	W/Op	Killed	Uden
Sgt	S J Malaband	MUG	Killed	Uden
Sgt	C E Scott	RG	Killed	Groesbeek

21st/22nd June 1944 Wesseling Lancaster LL955 ZN-E

P/O	J Brodie	P	Killed	Doornspijk
Sgt	F H Aldridge	FE	Killed	Doornspijk
F/Sgt	W Brownlee	Nav	Killed	Doornspijk
F/Sgt	D R N Keith	AB	Killed	Doornspijk
Sgt	R Sleep	W/Op	Killed	Doornspijk
P/O	R E Norton	MUG	Killed	Doornspijk
F/Sgt	G F L O'Connell	RG	Killed	Doornspijk

24/25th June 1944 Pommereval Lancaster LL975 ZN-H

P/O	S M Wright	P	Killed	St. Sever
Sgt	E S McPhail	FE	POW	
F/Sgt	H M Smith	Nav	Killed	St. Sever
Sgt	W R Knaggs	AB	POW	
F/Sgt	L J McGregor	W/Op	Killed	St. Sever
Sgt	A T Clark	MUG	Killed	St. Sever
F/Sgt	W Beutel	RG	Killed	St. Sever

27/28th June 1944 Vitry Lancaster JB664 ZN-N

P/O	N W Easby	P	Killed	Bransles
Sgt	E P Richomme	FE	Killed	Bransles
F/Sgt	A Robinson	Nav	Killed	Bransles
F/Sgt	J A G Dixon	AB	Killed	Bransles
Sgt	G A Collison	W/Op	Killed	Bransles
Sgt	L K Webb	MUG	Killed	Bransles
Sgt	D Hetherington	RG	Killed	Bransles

27/28th June 1944 Vitry Lancaster LL974 ZN-F

F/Sgt	E C Fox	P	Killed	Dieppe
Sgt	C H Southworth	FE	Killed	Dieppe
F/Sgt	A C Croft	Nav	Killed	Dieppe
Sgt	R Nelson	AB	Killed	Dieppe
Sgt	J D Pepper	W/Op	Killed	Dieppe
F/Sgt	M H Stoner	MUG	Killed	Dieppe
P/O	A E C Thomas	RG	Killed	Dieppe

4/5th July 1944 St. Leu D'Esserent Lancaster ND682 ZN-K

Sgt	E H Ekins	MUG	Killed	Walthamstow

Aircraft attacked by nightfighter enroute to target, F/O Mavaut landed safely at Woodbridge

4/5th July 1944 St. Leu D'Esserent Lancaster ND339 ZN-U

F/O	F Crosier	P	Killed	St. Sever
Sgt	R R Mosley	FE	Evaded	
F/Sgt	A G Ross	Nav	Evaded	
F/O	C A Price	AB	Evaded	
Sgt	T N Perara	W/Op	POW	
Sgt	W J Hardisty	MUG	Evaded	
Sgt	C L Churchyard	RG	POW	

4/5th July 1944 St. Leu D'Esserent Lancaster ME832 ZN-J

F/Sgt	S M Futcher	P	Killed	Runnymede
Sgt	R Bentley	FE	Killed	Marissel
F/Sgt	F H Stokeld	Nav	Killed	Marissel
F/Sgt	D McNaughton	AB	POW	
Sgt	J J Kearney	W/Op	Killed	Runnymede
F/O	W H Ramsey	MUG	Killed	Marissel
Sgt	A Bradley	RG	Killed	Marissel

7/8th July 1944 St. Leu D'Esserent Lancaster PB144 ZN-P

S/Ldr	T O Marshall	P	Killed	Marissel
P/O	G R Howell	FE	Killed	Marissel
F/O	I J Thompson	Nav	Killed	Marissel
Sgt	E G Banks	AB	Killed	Marissel
F/O	L C Zeffert	W/Op	Killed	St.Genevieve
F/O	J A Adams-Langley	MUG	Killed	St.Genevieve
F/O	P J O'Leary	RG	Killed	St.Genevieve

7/8th July 1944 St. Leu D'Esserent Lancaster ME668 ZN-L

F/O	G N Marchant	P	POW	
Sgt	F Wells	FE	POW	
F/O	W G Hardcastle	Nav	Killed	Eure st Loire
F/O	A G Kinnis	AB	POW	
W/O	H C Bell	W/Op	Killed	Runnymede
Sgt	W B Gladstone	MUG	Killed	Eure st Loire
F/O	F G Paterson	RG	Killed	Eure st Loire

7/8th July 1944 St. Leu D'Esserent Lancaster JB641 ZN-X

F/Sgt	F C Clement	P	Killed	St. Sever
Sgt	J M McLachlan	FE	Killed	St. Sever
F/O	W B Wilkinson	Nav	Killed	St. Sever
F/O	N V Gautschi	AB	Killed	St. Sever
Sgt	R D Potter	W/Op	Killed	St. Sever
Sgt	J Palmer	MUG	Killed	St. Sever
Sgt	J Balmer	RG	Killed	St. Sever

7/8th July 1944 St. Leu D'Esserent Lancaster ME831 ZN-R
P/O	A S Monaghan	P	Survived
Sgt	C F Swinley	FE	Evaded
F/Sgt	H G Philpot	Nav	Survived
Sgt	N C T Wand	AB	Survived
Sgt	G A Poulter	W/Op	Survived
Sgt	S F Gray	MUG	POW
Sgt	RK Sheridan	RG	Evaded

7/8th July 1944 St. Leu D'Esserent Lancaster ME789 ZN-R
F/O	G S Mather	P	POW
Sgt	J L Lucas	FE	POW
F/O	D A Evans	Nav	POW
F/O	J S Kingston	AB	POW
Sgt	W Stewart	W/Op	POW
Sgt	W Waldram	G	POW
Sgt	J Crawford	G	POW

28/29th July 1944 Stuttgart Lancaster ME778 ZN-O
P/O	L L Pemberton	P	Killed	Durnbach
Sgt	L Peace	FE	Killed	Durnbach
Sgt	J Newlands	Nav	Killed	Durnbach
F/O	A Clarkson	AB	Killed	Durnbach
Sgt	J H Morrison	W/Op	Killed	Durnbach
Sgt	J A J McGhie	MUG	Killed	Durnbach
Sgt	I Bowley	RG	Killed	Durnbach

30th July 1944 Cahagnes Lancaster PB304 ZN-S
F/O	P Lines	P	Killed	Runnymede
Sgt	R Barnes	FE	Killed	Runnymede
F/O	H Reid	Nav	Killed	Kirkwall
F/O	J H Steel	AB	Killed	Runnymede
Sgt	A W Young	W/Op	Killed	Runnymede
Sgt	J B Davenport	MUG	Killed	Sedgeley
Sgt	M Singh	RG	Killed	Golders Green

7th August 1944 Secqueville Lancaster LM641 ZN-P
F/O	G O Rabone	P	POW	
Sgt	K Buck	FE	POW	
F/O	A A Dilworth	Nav	POW	
F/O	S Bjarnason	AB	POW	
F/O	J Taylor	W/Op	Killed	Quetteville
Sgt	J MacNicol	MUG	POW	
Sgt	F G Ralph	RG	Killed	Quetteville

In the Middle of Nowhere - *The History of RAF Metheringham*

29/30th August 1944 Konigsberg Lancaster JB593 ZN-T

G/Cpt	W N McKechnie	P	Killed	Runnymede
P/O	R B Clarke	FE	Killed	Runnymede
F/Sgt	H W Carter	Nav	Killed	Runnymede
F/O	E E Fletcher	AB	Killed	Runnymede
Sgt	C C Jeffrey	W/Op	Killed	Runnymede
Sgt	D Forster	G	Killed	Runnymede
F/Sgt	E L Collins	G	Killed	Runnymede

29/30th August 1944 Konigsberg Lancaster ND331 ZN-G

F/O	L C W Boivin	P	Killed	Runnymede
Sgt	S Bell	FE	POW	
Sgt	W S Bryson	Nav	Killed	Runnymede
Sgt	J P Nicol	AB	POW	
F/Sgt	R H McLean	W/Op	Killed	Runnymede
Sgt	E G L Parker	MUG	Killed	Runnymede
Sgt	A Hargill	RG	Killed	Runnymede

11/12th September 1944 Darmstadt Lancaster PB203 ZN-M

F/Sgt	P R Mavaut	P	Killed	Runnymede
Sgt	F T James	FE	Killed	Runnymede
F/O	R L Kiteley	Nav	POW	
F/O	R L Montador	AB	POW	
Sgt	A Marlow	W/Op	Killed	Runnymede
P/O	L R Van Horne	G	Killed	Runnymede
P/O	G A Timothy	G	POW	

19/20th September 1944 Rheydt Lancaster PB347 ZN-G

F/O	A H Brindley	P	Killed	Reichswald
Sgt	R Litterick	FE	Killed	Reichswald
F/O	J Lloyd	Nav	Killed	Reichswald
F/O	K Ayres	AB	Survived	
W/O	L W Wheeler	W/Op	Killed	Reichswald
Sgt	P B Feltham	MUG	Killed	Reichswald
Sgt	RJ Chatwin	RG	Killed	Reichswald

19/20th September 1944 Rheydt Lancaster PB359 ZN-T

F/Lt	J Fee	P	POW	
Sgt	F G Treadgold	FE	POW	
Sgt	J E Brough	Nav	POW	
F/O	L J Darby	AB	Killed	Reichswald
F/O	G A Thompson	W/Op	Killed	Runnymede
F/O	J F V Marshall	MUG	Killed	Reichswald
Sgt	R Moscrop	RG	POW	

23/24 September 1944 Dortmund-Ems Lancaster ND868ZN-Q

F/Lt	S H Jones	P	POW?	
F/O	J Isaac	2nd P?	Killed	Reichswald
P/O	D Levene	FE	Killed	Reichswald
F/O	G G Bryan	Nav	Killed	Reichswald
P/O	H I Shepherd	AB	Killed	Reichswald
Sgt	R H Julian	W/Op	Killed	Reichswald
F/Sgt	J F Clarke	MUG	Killed	Reichswald
P/O	K A McLaughlin	RG	Killed	Reichswald

6/7 October 1944 Bremen Lancaster PD214 ZN-D

F/Lt	D Stewart	P	Killed	Runnymede
F/Sgt	J C Barlow	2nd P?	Killed	Becklingen
Sgt	R P Barton	FE	Killed	Runnymede
Sgt	G B Kirby	Nav	Killed	Runnymede
P/O	C J Service	AB	Killed	Runnymede
Sgt	G S Grogan	W/Op	Killed	Runnymede
Sgt	R J Paul	G	Killed	Becklingen
F/Sgt	J A Fell	G	Killed	Runnymede

1 November 1944 Homberg Lancaster PB303 ZN-R

F/O	G J Symes	P	Killed	Bergan Op Zoom
Sgt	A Harris	FE	Killed	Bergan Op Zoom
F/Sgt	C E Bayliss	Nav	Killed	Bergan Op Zoom
F/O	J A Smith	AB	Killed	Bergan Op Zoom
F/O	L W Perry	W/Op	Killed	Bergan Op Zoom
Sgt	J A Crisp	G	Killed	Bergan Op Zoom
F/Sgt	C E L Cook	G	Killed	Bergan Op Zoom

6/7 November 1944 Mittleland Canal Lancaster LL953 ZN-O

F/O	C D Neale	P	Killed	Reichswald
Sgt	R L Armstrong	FE	Killed	Reichswald
F/Sgt	W Hardy	Nav	Killed	Reichswald
F/Sgt	S N Hilder	AB	Killed	Reichswald
Sgt	W M McIntyre	W/Op	Killed	Reichswald
Sgt	W Clyde	MUG	Killed	Reichswald
Sgt	J M Croll	RG	Killed	Reichswald

4/5 December 1944 Heilbronn Lancaster PB281 ZN-J
F/O	H J Thompson	P	Killed	Durnbach
Sgt	H S Sands	FE	Killed	Durnbach
W/O	N M Menzies	Nav	Killed	Durnbach
F/Sgt	D E Hanscombe	AB	Killed	Durnbach
F/Sgt	D G Allbon	W/Op	Killed	Durnbach
F/Sgt	G R McCullum	MUG	Killed	Durnbach
F/Sgt	L P Burton	RG	Survived	

15/16 December 1944 Baltic (Mining) Lancaster ND682 ZN-X
F/O	E Barratt	P	Killed	Halsingborg
Sgt	J F W Emerson	FE	Killed	Anholt
F/Sgt	A Berry	Nav	Killed	Runnymede
F/Sgt	E G Towle	AB	Killed	Runnymede
F/Sgt	C P Calvert	W/Op	Killed	Runnymede
Sgt	R E Day	G	Killed	Runnymede
Sgt	P E Green	G	Killed	Runnymede

18/19 December 1944 Gydnia Lancaster NN726 ZN-D
F/Lt	M S F Pritchard	P	Killed	Marlbork
Sgt	E W Skipper	FE?	Killed	Marlbork
F/Sgt	F J Turkentine	Nav?	Killed	Marlbrok
F/O	P F Croft	AB	Killed	Marlbrok
F/Sgt	S Robinson	W/Op	Killed	Marlbrok
Sgt	R Egglestone	MUG	POW	
Sgt	H Ainley	RG	POW	

4/5 January 1945 Royan Lancaster PB617 ZN-B
F/O	A H Scott	P	Killed	St.Palais sur Mer
Sgt	P A Lane	FE	Killed	St.Palais sur Mer
F/O	B T Roberts	Nav	Killed	St.Palais sur Mer
F/O	V D Powell	AB	Killed	St.Palais sur Mer
F/O	C A Cassidy	W/Op	Killed	St.Palais sur Mer
F/Sgt	P W K Waller	MUG	Killed	St.Palais sur Mer
F/Sgt	C R Mangnall	RG	Killed	St.Palais sur Mer

7/8 January 1945 Munich Lancaster PB724 ZN-L
F/O	J N Scott	P	Killed	Choloy
Sgt	L D Knapman	FE	Killed	Choloy
F/O	K C Darke	Nav	Killed	Choloy
F/O	R D Dunlop	AB	Killed	Choloy
Sgt	H J Stunnell	W/Op	POW	
Sgt	J F Elson	MUG	Killed	Choloy
Sgt	R B Needle	RG	POW	

14/15 January 1945 Leuna Lancaster PB122 ZN-Y

F/O	D R McIntosh	P	Killed	St.Sever
Sgt	F A Kendall	FE	Killed	St.Sever
F/Sgt	R A Quiney	Nav	Killed	St.Sever
F/Sgt	R H Thomson	AB	Killed	St.Sever
F/Sgt	W H Butt	W/Op	Killed	St.Sever
Sgt	G Fletcher	G	Killed	St.Sever
Sgt	D S Ford	G	Killed	St.Sever

11 March 1945 Metheringham HurricaneII PZ740

P/O	Parlato	P	Killed

12 March 1945 Dortmund Lancaster RA508 ZN-B

P/O	F E Baker	P	Killed	Runnymede
Sgt	D Y Carter	FE	Killed	Runnymede
F/Sgt	H G Harding	Nav	Killed	Runnymede
F/Sgt	W J Cooper	AB	Killed	Runnymede
F/Sgt	G P O'Brien	W/Op	Killed	Runnymede
Sgt	K R Haw	G	Killed	Runnymede
Sgt	H Gillender	G	Killed	Runnymede

14/15 March 1945 Lutzkendorf Lancaster LL948 ZN-V

F/O	B E Barrow	P	Killed	Runnymede
Sgt	H Castle	FE	Killed	Runnymede
F/Sgt	H Bedford	Nav	Killed	Runnymede
W/O	J B Cossart	AB	Killed	Runnymede
F/Sgt	R K Locke	W/Op	Killed	Runnymede
Sgt	G H Armstrong	MUG	Killed	Runnymede
Sgt	J S Hussey	RG	POW	

In the Middle of Nowhere - *The History of RAF Metheringham*